An Unstoppable Runner

David Williams

An Unstoppable Runner

For my beautiful and loving wife Dale, as well as our four wonderful children – Steve, Vicki, Julia and Heather.
Thank you for all your love and support in my running and everything else

and

in loving memory of Allison

An Unstoppable Runner
ISBN 978 1 76109 163 6
Copyright © text David Williams 2021
Cover photo: Lynne Santamaria

First published 2021 by
Ginninderra Press
PO Box 3461 Port Adelaide 5015
www.ginninderrapress.com.au

Contents

Foreword		7
1	Ready, Steady, Go	9
2	Becoming Inspired	17
3	A Marathon Effort	23
4	Diving Into the World of Ultras	31
5	Pushing My Limits	37
6	Running For Charity	42
7	Heading to the Desert	53
8	The Gibbers Strike	61
9	Down the Trail	69
10	Running In Circles	74
11	Beyond My Limits	82
12	Rumble in the Jungle	88
13	The Edge of the World	96
14	Reality Bites	99
15	A Runner's Musings	111
16	Long May We Run	119
17	The Pain Cave	125
18	Food For Thought	130
19	A Time to Learn	138
20	Hanging in There	144
21	Booked to Run	151
22	The End of the Trail?	155
23	Mirror, Mirror, on the Wall	162
Appendix		164
Acknowledgements		166
About the Author		168

As you set out for Ithaka
hope your road is a long one,
full of adventure, full of discovery.

Keep Ithaka always in your mind.
Arriving there is what you're destined for.
But don't hurry the journey at all.
Better if it lasts for years,
so you're old by the time you reach the island,
wealthy with all you have gained on the way,
not expecting Ithaka to make you rich.

From 'Ithaka' by C.P. Cavafy

Foreword

A lot of people run to win medals, to set records, to continuously run faster and finish first, but ultra runners go beyond all that to discover what being first really is. In *An Unstoppable Runner*, David Williams has been able to tap into the very core of an ultra runner's motivation, to discover who they really are and to whom. David relays his steel-forged strength and his ability to cope with disaster through the fires of running. An unstoppable runner is one who has found a higher purpose, an awakening and an understanding of who they are and what they must be to find fulfillment. *An Unstoppable Runner* teaches us that somewhere, near the threshold of pain and failure, comes the realisation that a life without barriers or borders is true freedom. Somewhere, just beyond pain, comes euphoria and knowing that even the most ordinary of us can be great.

In this book, David Williams takes us on a journey to many countries and climates through decades of time, to prove that we were meant to run the corners of this world and experience every aspect of life. To anyone who is wondering who they are or what they should be, David says, simply go for a run, a long run and eventually you will discover the answers. The peace and solitude that now surrounds David on Flinders Island is fitting, considering his journey through the trails, deserts and highways of this manic world an ultra runner calls home.

Pat Farmer AM

Sharing a race with son Steve.

The island community supporting a charity run.

In the wilds of Cambodia.

With running buddies at Tarawera.

Great support in Launceston–Hobart run.

A happy end to a marathon.

1

Ready, Steady, Go

'Man cannot discover new oceans unless he has the courage to lose sight of the shore.' – Andre Gide

Forty years ago, I chanced upon running. Since then, it has meant so much more than just exercise. To me, the act of running for five or six days a week has been therapeutic and life-changing. I am who I am today in a large part because of my daily runs. How fortunate I was to find it.

Of course it hasn't all been easy. There have been abject failures among the glorious successes along the way but I hope that this book, which takes you on my journey, warts and all, will show that it doesn't take an extraordinary person to achieve things they had thought beyond them.

When I first started to write, I had not intended to say much about my childhood days since, in reading other runners' books, it sometimes appeared to be unnecessary 'small stuff'. But, looking back as the Old Fart Runner (OFR) that I am now, I have come to see that those early days were the crucible from which my adult life and passions were forged.

My very earliest running experience was when I was probably around five years old. I can't remember whether it was with my brother or a friend, but we loved playing Knock Down Ginger (why it was called that I've never known), which meant knocking loudly on the door of some local elderly person and then legging it down the road at full throttle, before they could open the door to find nobody there.

Looking back, I can see that this was a pretty mean thing to do but I recall laughing until I got the hiccups as we fled down the street.

I grew up near a small village in the south of England, spending every spare hour possible out in the hills and woods that surrounded our house. Mum and Dad were strict at home but allowed me the freedom to do pretty much what I wanted outdoors. I collected birds' eggs, went on long exploratory bike rides, built camps near streams and generally ran a little wild. As an adult, something of those early days must have stayed with me because, when I eventually found myself running or hiking deep in the Australian bush, it felt a lot like going home (not to England but within myself).

My early sporting endeavours were limited to playing cricket for my school and later our local village team. My dad was a wonderful batsman and from the earliest age he was my hero. I was desperate to follow in his footsteps. For years, I was an opening left-handed batsman and loved the game for all it was worth. As a teenager, I took lessons at indoor cricket nets during the dreary cold English winters, with a dream of one day playing professionally for our local county, Sussex. Such hopes disappeared into smoke, as I grew up too small in stature and bulk for such ambitions to become reality. Unbeknown to me at the time, however, it was a body more suited to long-distance running than withstanding the might of fast bowlers.

I was an introverted boy who wanted to be liked by everyone but felt unable to step forward and make friendships. I always seemed to be standing on the outside of any group, spending much of my free time alone in the countryside. My favourite spot was an Iron Age fort known as Cissbury Ring that was perched high on the South Downs about two kilometres from our home. There, I could ride my bike, fly home-made model airplanes, or simply lie hidden in the sweet-smelling grass and watch the toothpaste-white cumulus clouds scud across the sky.

The boys' high school that I attended from the age of eleven was in Worthing, a small seaside resort. It was a somewhat shabby town, sort of worn at the edges and quite a windy spot, with salt-laden air, where older folk came for their brief annual holidays in faded bed and breakfast accommodation. The beaches were large banks of pebbles that rattled as they were pushed and pulled by the chilly grey waves. Swimming was for the brave or foolhardy.

The school itself was a wooden structure built, I think, as an army training camp during the Second World War. The external cladding was creosoted every couple of years and, as we walked the quadrangles between classes, our nostrils were assaulted with that pungent smell.

The playing fields surrounding the school were big enough for two cricket matches to be played simultaneously and they kept my sporting ambitions satisfied in the summer months. The long, wet and windy winters, however, were a different kettle of fish. The official winter sport of Worthing High School for Boys was rugby football. Unfortunately, I was too small and skinny to be even worth considering for a position in any of the school sides so, when I was fifteen, our sports master, Peter Benson, talked me into 'volunteering' for the school cross-country team. As far as I can remember, we didn't have inter-school competitions but being on the team made you eligible for the County Junior Championship.

Our Wednesday training runs always seemed to be on wet, windy afternoons and usually didn't venture anywhere near a field or trail. Instead, we had to run a circuit on streets around the school, before enduring a cold shower in unheated change rooms. It wasn't exactly an ideal introduction to long-distance running.

As with everything else I did, I took training for the 1962 County Under 16 event pretty seriously. Other than our weekly school run of around five kilometres, I would head over to our local park after school and run a few laps. I didn't have any concept of what I was doing – just believing that I had to run more if I was to be competitive. I don't think anyone gave me any advice; I just did it. And I did it in an old pair of dirty white plimsolls (sneakers). Not the best choice, but I didn't know any different and it was clearly before the 'jogger' era arrived.

Just before the championship, however, a family friend donated a snazzy pair of track spikes. The uppers were fancy crimson leather and I fell in love with them straight away, but I soon realised that even walking in them required a very different step. They were made more uncomfortable by being slightly too small for my feet, which meant that I couldn't wear socks, so I elected not to wear the spikes until race day. Of course, years later, I could see what a huge mistake that was. When I now see a pair of new shoes on anyone at the start of an event, it always makes me smile as I remember 1962.

The big day came around and it was on a typically cold, wet and windy November morning that my dad took me to the starting area, an hour's drive from home. It had snowed the previous day and there were patches of slush lying under some of the trees and bushes around the course. In the race, we had to push through some muddy sections and at one point I slipped into an icy stream swollen with the recent snow and rain. By the finish, I was gasping for breath, chilled through with wet clothes and could feel how my ill-fitting 'new' shoes had brought on a couple of large open heel blisters. I finished somewhere near the middle of the field and, having given the race my all, I came to the disappointing conclusion that I was not cut out for such athletic endeavours.

Sadly, it was to be many years before I was to enter another race of that nature. I guess that, being a fully fledged adolescent, I had other things on my mind. Things might have been different if my school had had a greater focus on athletics. There was certainly no track season as such and no after-school training to provide encouragement for a runner of any distance. Funnily enough, they did hold an annual sports day and I was always chosen by my house to run the track mile. My performances must have been totally unforgettable given that that is *all* I can recall.

So it was that my slide into adulthood was totally devoid of focused running pursuits. I continued to play team sports with a passion but, when I discovered the delights of individual sport, it was golf that I followed my dad into.

My running career, or perhaps 'my running days' is a more accurate phrase, really started when I lived in the British colony of Hong Kong. I went there in 1976, with my first wife, to work for an international firm of accountants, whose office was in a rather grand building next door to the classy Mandarin Hotel. Most days, we would repair to their restaurant for a somewhat boisterous and boozy lunch. If that wasn't bad enough for my health, I joined the Kowloon Cricket Club, where I met a fine group of fellows who enjoyed living life to the hilt. It didn't take much encouragement for me to go along with them. Coming from a quiet existence in suburban England, it was all new and exciting.

Our cricket team, the Saracens, played Saturday afternoons but we would practise for an hour every evening after work, and then spend some hours in the snooker room, sampling the local San Miguel beer. Sometimes, it was extremely late when the taxi dropped me outside my flat. Occasionally, I was sober enough to remember getting out of the taxi.

On top of all this, I was expected to entertain business clients visiting the colony, which always included more booze and, sometimes, topless bars in the seedy part of town. Such dissolute times couldn't continue without disastrous results. At thirty-two, I was becoming podgy about the waist and my disgusting smoking habit was weighing heavily on me. I could feel myself slipping down into a bottomless pit and I knew that I had to shape up. Of course, that was easier said than done when your workmates and friends led a similarly dissolute lifestyle.

In this regard, I shall always remain indebted to a young Scottish solicitor named Mackie Brander, with whom I worked on joint clients' cases. Mackie was a lean and long-standing runner. He had run a marathon or two and was, therefore, somewhat of a hero in my eyes. He enthused about the benefits of running and encouraged me to buy my first pair of joggers, start exercising and take control of my health. The joggers were a tacky brown pair of Adidas bought from a large Chinese emporium, somewhere among the maze of lanes in Hong Kong's central district. They were possessed of minimal cushioning and probably not the greatest choice, but I reckoned they looked great. I felt very proud to be racing off down the road wearing them together with a brilliant blue satin pair of shorts with white trim and a baggy T-shirt advertising the local beer.

It was the commencement of a lifetime love affair with running and a simple time that I will always look back on fondly.

Instead of going to the cricket club every evening, I would head home to the small seaside village of Stanley. Putting on my running garb, I would race flat out for two or three kilometres, in typically humid conditions, trying hard to beat my time of the previous day. After every evening run, I staggered in the door with sweat streaming out of every pore, feeling exhausted, but elated at what I was doing. Of course, going as fast as I could every day wasn't a good idea and it soon led to some minor injuries and constant colds. My friend Mackie listened to my sob story and patiently explained the principles and benefits of Long, Slow Distance, lending me Jim Fixx's masterpiece *The Complete Book of Running*. What an eye-opener that book was. It showed me what the benefits of daily running at an easier pace could be and there was something in Fixx's writing style that captivated me. The simple sketched illustrations also made me want to get out there and go for a run.

I consumed it in a couple of evenings and have been addicted to running and reading about it ever since. I couldn't believe that I had wasted my previous years not running. What had I been thinking about for thirty-two years? I found that I just loved going out in the heat and humidity that is Hong Kong for a long slow run. For me, there has always been something therapeutic and cleansing about running in oppressive conditions. I think it must have something to do with the almost sauna-like effect on my body as well as my mind. And the feeling when I have finished and taken a long cool shower is one of great well-being.

At the time, I didn't give any thought as to why I was running, just that it gave me pleasure. I had certainly started because of the way my health was deteriorating but there was no reason to believe that it would become so important over the years.

People have sometimes asked, half jokingly, what it is that I'm running away from. I don't feel as though I'm running away from anything. On the contrary, I seem to be running *towards* a better lifestyle and a more positive outlook on everything, with greater energy to do those things. If the average person in Australia has a life expectancy of around thirty thousand days, it seems important that I make the most of such a limited supply. And perhaps running will even extend that limit.

It wasn't long before I discovered that Hong Kong Island, and the New Territories on the mainland, were covered with a network of beautiful rocky and wild trails and that one of them started almost next door to my flat. That trail took me in zigzag fashion up a steep hill, shaded by trees festooned with brilliant green creepers, onto a rugged track with many steps that had originally connected two remote villages. It was rough enough to cause me to stumble regularly but the beauty was that, in the crazy rushed world that was (and still is) Hong Kong, I was alone. Just my thoughts and me.

It certainly sounds like a contradiction in terms, Hong Kong and countryside, let alone solitude, but it was exciting to find and explore those connecting paths off the beaten track. In many places, I was surprised to find them tucked away just metres away from high-rise blocks of flats in the Mid-Levels residential areas.

It was after work, on one of those trail outings, that I happened to bump into my dentist, who was also out for a run. He explained that the next evening there was a Hash House Harriers meeting and suggested that I went along. The Hash, as it is commonly referred to, meets every week in many, many places around the world and runs over a marked course of about five kilometres. Since there is a fair bit of beer drunk afterwards, the Hash is laughingly talked about as a drinking club with a running problem. So I fitted in immediately. Very quickly, this group formed a large part of my social life for the remainder of my stay in the former colony, until it was time to move down to Sydney, where I had been offered a really good job.

While the Hash was a great social environment in which to run, it became clear that I needed to improve my training on the other weekdays. So I adopted a stricter programme, using Jim Fixx's book as a guide, and, with some hard effort, established a solid base on which I could build in the future. And the benefits of regular exercise impacted positively on all aspects of my life. Instead of heading to the bar after cricket practice at the Kowloon Cricket Club, I would run a few laps around the ground, enjoy a fresh lemon juice and drive home.

In a way, it was a bit of a relief to escape from Hong Kong. It had been an exciting time in the period from 1976 to 1980, but the colony was rapidly changing. When I first arrived, the Old China Hands, as the expatriates who had lived there a long time were known, still behaved as though they were entitled to live elevated lives and treated the local Chinese in a pretty bad way. The rest of us, the younger shorter-term expats, were more accepting of the equality of our position among the locals but, even so, we did have certain privileges and did indeed earn more than our local equivalents.

After the Chinese ruler Mao Tse-tung died in 1979, however, things started to change rapidly. The Western world began to move into China big time. Major US companies, of which Coca Cola and McDonalds constituted the obvious forerunners, were getting a foothold. The residents of Hong Kong became concerned about their future. Would they remain independent or become a small part of China, with little autonomy?

The expatriate influence was lessening, while the pace of everyday life seemed to be ratcheting up a notch, so my escape to Sydney in April 1980 was a great relief to me.

2

Becoming Inspired

'I often hear someone say I'm not a real runner. We are all runners, some just faster than the others. I never met a fake runner.' – Bart Yasso

Other than my arrival, 1980 was a pretty quiet sort of year in Australia. The world was in turmoil over the upcoming Moscow Olympic Games as a result of the Soviet Union's invasion of Afghanistan. Malcolm Fraser was prime minister and Evonne Cawley (née Goolagong) won her second Wimbledon singles final.

My new home in Sydney immediately felt quietly civilised and attractive after the hurly-burly of Asia. I looked around the leaf-lined suburbs, the gleaming harbour and the magnificent old sandstone buildings in the city, and felt at home almost straight away.

The office that I went to work in was slap bang in the middle of the city. In my first lunch break, I was amazed to see crowds of young people in running gear emerging from different offices, heading down towards the harbour front. Coming from such a crowded, polluted place as Hong Kong, this was quite something to behold and held glorious dreams for the future.

I was very fortunate that one of my new work colleagues was also a keen runner. Sometimes, it has felt like fate has taken me on this lifetime journey of running. Every step of the way, I have found people who have shared the love and freedom of running.

My new-found buddy, Bob Mann, and I took off most lunchtimes to run round the Sydney Botanical Gardens, which since the early

1980s have been a real running mecca in the city. We would enter through the gigantic wrought-iron gates next to the Sydney Opera House and follow a sealed footpath around the cove to Lady Macquarie's Chair (in reality, this was just a weathered alcove in a sandstone rock face, with a ledge to sit upon). Usually, we'd meet up with others we had got to know over the years and run a quite hard six or seven kilometres, do some stair repeats or even head out along the northern harbour foreshore after crossing the 'coathanger' bridge.

That route took us into some beautiful bush trails on Sydney's north shore, but usually meant that we were out for more than our allotted hour and got us into a little strife now and then. Hot and sweaty, we'd grab a quick shower in the shabby and quite putrid basement of our building before getting back to our desks, trying to act like we'd been out of the office for a quick bite to eat. Our red faces and dripping hair always gave us away and our boss was never too impressed by our absences. He was of the school that believed you were meant to take clients out for big lunches or just spend the time working at your desk.

Day by day, my running was making me leaner and fitter. I began to read and hear about local races and wondered what it would be like to test myself in one or two. I finally bit the bullet and nervously entered a five-kilometre road race just down the road from where I lived. It felt very strange to be lined up with such a large number of runners and I didn't want to let myself down by running too slowly.

I guess that a bit of ego came into it as I pushed hard from the word go, giving it my best shot, and crossed the finish line totally wrecked. Looking round afterwards, I could see only a crowd of smiling, contented people all bubbling with excitement about the race. I had tasted something quite exquisite. From being just an individual runner, I could see that I was now on the edge of a huge inclusive club, the global running community.

So, gradually, gradually, my life became inextricably entwined with running. At that time, I was married with two small children, so was limited to what I could do, but I certainly pushed the envelop. One of the outcomes of the integration of running as a major factor in my lifestyle was that, although I enjoyed working hard and took pride in doing it well, I had limited ambitions for job advancement. It just wasn't that important in the scheme of things as I saw it. A job was a means to earn the income I needed to live the way I wanted to, and running was a large part of that.

Perhaps it was the dislike of the suburban daily grind of a long day's work, a lot of travel to and fro, eating, sleeping and then repeating it all endlessly that eventually shaped my ambition to live on a peaceful island away from such a draining lifestyle.

But I am getting ahead of myself. It is still 1981. Oblivious to outside factors, I was fit and focused on races, forever training for the next big thing. After that first eye-opening five-kilometre race, I entered several more around Sydney, enjoying every minute but I also had one eye on the challenge of longer distances. At first, ten kilometres seemed to be my limit and I would enjoy travelling to distant suburbs most Sundays to test myself. Later on, I would use races of that distance for speed work but back then it was simply a weekly fulfilment of my running passion.

The fourteen-kilometre City to Surf occupied an important annual goal for a few years before the crowds became so great that you couldn't really call it a race, unless you were one of the elite, and I was certainly not in that bracket. But in the early days it was a lot of fun. The first time I entered that event in 1981, I found bands playing along the course, and there was a general party atmosphere everywhere with boisterous barbecues held on front lawns. Offers of an adult drink or slices of oranges came every now and then along the way.

While it was a fun run and I enjoyed it as such, there came a time when I wanted to move upwards again in distance and perhaps take things a little more seriously. Of course, as an OFR, I now realise that there is room for every kind of running event in our lives – but back then I felt very strongly that running should not be taken lightly.

I kept careful records of my race times, with all the certificates going into a scrapbook that I still have. Breaking my PB for each distance was important. I didn't have any grandiose expectations of myself or want to measure myself against anybody else, but just wanted to see what I could achieve. At a basic level, I guess that I simply loved the feeling I got from pushing myself hard in training as well as races.

After a couple of years, I was more than ready to step up to a half marathon. There were several halves around Sydney at the time and I had a lot of fun running in a few. Probably the best and most challenging was held in the lovely Lane Cove National Park, which had some pretty tough hills. Like runners of all abilities around the world, I wanted to know what my limits were. So I threw myself into becoming adept at racing half marathons, managing to break ninety minutes – once and once only.

I think it was my workmate, Bob, who first brought up the idea of running a marathon. This was in 1982 and the 42.2-kilometre event was just growing in the imagination of Australian runners. Robert De Castella ('Deeks') was a young rising star and we lesser mortals were being inspired by him and his achievements. *Runners World* magazine was also exhorting us to get out there and do amazing things. Entering a marathon wasn't an overnight decision but, rather, it just crept up on me like an incoming tide. There was a distinct inevitability about it, tinged with an element of fear.

Signing up for the 1982 Legal & General marathon felt very different from previous races. I was extremely aware of the enormity of the jump from a half to a full marathon. In those days, the fields were small and it seemed to me that only elite athletes could actually finish, or even consider entering, such an arduous race. Hardly anyone I spoke to outside of my running circle seemed to know about, and certainly did not care about, such things that were so far out of their sphere of interest.

But perhaps it was the fact that marathons and their more extreme relations, ultra marathons, were seen to be out of the ordinary that I was attracted to them. Caught up in the passion of it all, I committed myself totally to training and running that 1982 marathon. My emerging obsessiveness should have been a warning to me of what the future held, but ignorance is bliss.

One lunchtime, on my way to the Botanical Gardens, I ran the short distance from my workplace to the Legal & General Insurance city offices and, feeling very self-conscious, collected a blank entry form. Of course there was no Internet at that time and entries were submitted by post. So you were never really sure about entry until your race package arrived in the mail. It was then an exciting wait for the big race day to arrive.

My training was a fairly haphazard affair loosely based on a programme I found in the well-thumbed pages of *Runners World*. Although very apprehensive about this first attempt at a marathon, I was quite naive and didn't put in enough long runs in the lead-up to the race.

The event was set for an autumn Sunday morning along Sydney's north shore, finishing at the pretty beach of Manly. Norfolk Pines lined the route along the promenade to the finish banner, like a row of huge green umbrellas. There were quite a few hills along the course that took their toll on me. An unseasonal heat also played its part, but I managed to cross the finish line in a little over four hours, after falling into a very big hole of pain around the thirty-five-kilometre mark (which I later found out was known as 'hitting the wall').

Looking back on that race and, indeed, on many of the seventy-odd marathons that I ran over the next few years, it seems hard to believe that I was so blissfully unaware of the need for proper nutrition and hydration. It was not something commonly discussed back in the day. I seemed to survive on water and a Mars bar or two in most of the marathons I ran. Occasionally, the organisers offered such delights as Gatorade, but mostly it was just plain old water at the aid stations.

No wonder I had some spectacular glycogen crashes in those early days when I pushed myself hard, causing me to hit that proverbial wall far too often. As well as muscular exhaustion, my brain would turn to mush, so that I was incapable of any clear logical thoughts. On one occasion, I couldn't even follow the simplest of directions being given by a volunteer near the finish line. Gels, salt tablets and energy bars were all in the distant future; what I would have given for them back in 1982.

There were probably only about two hundred men and women in that Legal & General marathon so we became fairly spread out and I didn't see too many people along the route, other than the kindly folk operating the few obligatory aid stations. Certainly there were no spectators save for groups of family and friends at the finish; so very different from modern events. My time of just over four hours didn't bother me, I simply felt very proud of myself in achieving a long-held dream. I was now a marathoner.

In the days following the race, it took quite a while for my legs to recover and for me to be mentally ready for more but, in any event, my first marathon had been a real revelation. For many people, running just one marathon is enough, but I had tested the water and wanted to jump in and do it again. And again.

Crossing the finish line of that first marathon certainly transformed me. From that point on, running long distances was cemented as a central part of my life and has remained so to this day as an OFR, despite all the setbacks. I would be lying if I said that this didn't have an impact on my family life, especially when Vicki and Steve were small. They wanted attention over the weekends when I was committed to my long runs and couldn't be home as much as I should have been. I tried my best to be a good father but with 20/20 hindsight I certainly recognise that I was somewhat selfish in my outlook.

3

A Marathon Effort

'Far better is it to dare mighty things, to win glorious triumphs, even though checked by failure...than to rank with those spirits who neither enjoy nor suffer much because they live in a grey twilight that knows not victory nor defeat.' – Theodore Roosevelt

With the increased importance of running came the realisation that I needed to be more focused about putting in the long runs. They held the key to success in marathons. Up to then, I have to admit that, although desperately keen, I was somewhat undisciplined in my approach. I just ran whatever I felt like on the day. Especially now, as an Old Fart Runner, I fully understand the importance of having a structured approach to training, if I want to be the best I can be.

It was in 1982 that the running group Sydney Striders became an important part of my running life. One of the people I had spoken to at my first five-kilometre event was an organiser of this newly formed running group. He explained that every week the Striders held a STAR (Sunday Training Run) on a different route through a wide variety of suburbs for distances of up to thirty kilometres, a lot more than I was currently doing. Before heading out each Sunday, every runner was handed a map printed from the Sydney road directory, with meticulous directions on the back.

After having trained mostly on my own for so long, it was great fun running with a group of twelve or more people, from all walks of life, whom I got to know better each week. There was a child psychologist, a few advertising executives, a gardener and a male nurse among them.

And, of course, doing anything in a group environment always provides additional motivation. There were fast, medium and slow groups available to run with, but the starting times varied, so that the entire club met up at the finish for a social breakfast at a member's house.

One of the regular members was the well-known author Bryce Courtney, who used to talk at length about his writing, particularly the development of his characters. His first novel, *The Power of One*, was a special case in point, as he would explain how stuck he had become in writing the ending, but he just loved talking out loud about it all. Chatting to people like Bryce made those long runs much more enjoyable and helped to take my mind off the physical demand of them.

With such great companionship, I soon found that I was able to increase my distances and, in time, get a bit quicker. I moved up from the slow to the medium group – they both had the same philosophy, but the medium group got to eat breakfast a little earlier.

I would rock up to their meets every Sunday morning wherever they were. As it usually meant getting out of bed around five a.m. in order to arrive at the selected start in time for the slow group, it also meant a particularly quiet Saturday evening and an early night, much to my first wife's chagrin.

Sydney is a beautiful place in which to run, as there are many hidden trails and parks to explore; places you'd not ordinarily see. Because the spreading suburbs couldn't invade some of the steeper bush areas, local councils chose them as ideal places to keep 'green' and they all seemed to have trails carved through them. The STARs incorporated these trails as much as possible and they brought a pleasant break from road running.

I remember one glorious summer Sunday morning run from Bondi Beach along the coastal path heading south. It was one of the Striders' most popular STARs, as it was a pure coastal run with a swim in the pristine surfing waters of Bondi afterwards. Imagine my surprise when a small group of us turned a corner and were crossing a piece of parkland to see a totally naked woman stroll right in front of us, walking a dog on a leash. I'm afraid that I can't remember what breed of dog it was. The lady didn't blink an eye, although I certainly did, and it put a stop to our conversation for a while.

Over the next year I gradually built up to a thirty-kilometre run with the medium-paced group every Sunday that put me in an ideal position to venture forth into more and more marathons. The weekly long run was working its magic. By 1986, when I was nearing forty, I was going along pretty well, managing to avoid any substantial injury and entering loads of marathons. But I realised that if I wanted to improve my times, I had to make even further adjustments to my training.

Accordingly, I took advice from a book and started to incorporate more speed work and hill running into my regime. Over a six-week period, this increased workload saw a measurable increase in my speed over long distances and I saw a little bit of surplus weight drop from my already pretty scrawny body. I felt ready to put it to the test in the 1986 Canberra Marathon.

I stood on the start line feeling nervous but my body was more than ready to face the day. Our capital city is a fine place to run a marathon PB. The looped course is flat and the weather in April is usually ideal; sunny but cool, especially in the early morning. I completed the first loop strongly with loads of energy in my legs, but towards the completion of the race I could feel the lactic acid building up and was delighted to cross the finish line in 3.08. I was exhausted from giving it my all, but extremely elated at this personal best and getting so close to the magical three-hour mark, which average runners like myself often see as the ultimate goal. As a result of pushing myself so hard in that race, it took me more than a week before I could again run decently. By then, I had a whiff of an even faster time and dreamt of breaking through that three-hour barrier.

After thinking about this and chatting to other runners who were more experienced than myself, I decided to increase my mileage at my optimal marathon pace and add some even more intense speed work into the mix. I entered a few half marathons, using them to measure my speed improvements. Although I managed to creep under one and a half hours for twenty-one kilometres, I was very conscious of the huge gap between half and full marathons. To fill that gap, I pushed harder and harder.

Unfortunately, I didn't know then what I know now as an OFR and what I wish I had known back then. I cobbled together another six-week training schedule with tempo runs, speed and hill work as well as long runs (thirty-kilometre plus) at a three-hour marathon pace. I ignored the idea of rest days, wanting to use every possible opportunity of improving. I even joined a gym and did weight training three or four times a week, concentrating on my legs of course.

Needless to say, trying too hard every day, every week, caused me to break down. I struggled with continuous and various niggling injuries. Because I was pushing my training to the limit, I soon became somewhat rundown health-wise, catching every cold and flu bug going the rounds. I was mentally drained from all the effort and became generally quite depressed at what seemed like a downturn in my running career. Whereas I had hoped to take a step up, I found myself heading back towards the basement level of running.

In running clubs like the Sydney Striders, there is always somebody faster than you. Without consciously thinking about it, I had tried to keep up with those going a little too fast for me and, when I managed to do so, lo and behold there was yet another person with even greater speed. I certainly didn't feel like I was being competitive, just trying to be the best runner I possibly could be. Even so, it gradually dawned on me that this was not the way I should be going.

Being forced out of action through an injury, I had time to think about what running meant to me, and what I should be focusing on to get the most out of the sport. After all, let's face it: I was doing it purely for pleasure. Sure, I needed to see what I was capable of achieving but, perhaps, the search should be for something more meaningful than a sub-three-hour marathon.

A couple of my Strider mates found themselves in a similar position. The three of us mused about the issue during several long Sunday runs and eventually decided that, instead of trying to get faster, we'd simply run more marathons at a decent and more sustainable pace. In turn, this would be more fun but still represent a challenge to each of us. After all, it was the running of marathons themselves that turned us on, the buzz we got from a morning's hard effort and being around like-minded people.

So that's what we did; we entered as many events as we could find. Sometimes we were racing three marathons on successive weekends. The three of us travelled around the eastern seaboard of Australia, collecting medals and T-shirts from an amazing variety of places and races with strange names like 'Fisher's Ghost'. We were relaxed on the start line, splashed each other in puddles we passed, threw sponges and other childlike deeds, having an absolute ball, laughing and joking through 42.2 kilometres.

Being so relaxed engendered a positive approach to every race. Sure, pain always paid a visit but, keeping any negative thoughts at bay, I was able to finish them all in good nick. An added bonus was that I got home about lunchtime with more energy to play with the kids.

Over the next two or three years, I chalked up nearly seventy marathons, most of which were completed steadily in around three hours thirty minutes. By adopting this more casual approach to my running, I stopped getting injured and was in pretty good health most of the time. With all those races in my calendar, it meant that I couldn't train much in between them, just recover, jog for a couple of lunchtimes and be ready for the following weekend. It was an exhilarating time and I wasn't looking beyond the next few marathons.

Many of the races had a very social 'carbo-loading' pasta dinner the night before. And if there was no organised event, a few of us would head out to an Italian restaurant for a meal instead. It was fun to relax with some friends pre-race and those get-togethers increased the pleasure I was getting from the overall marathon experience.

Gradually, however, the enthusiasm paled, as indeed it must when you're doing the same old thing over and over again. After all, one road marathon differs very little from another, especially when I was running the same ones year after year. It seemed natural to start looking for alternative events in the running world. I found them in the hidden world of ultra marathons. Back then, only a few ultras existed and they were somehow 'underground', like a subversive society hidden from the mainstream world. Whenever you spoke to runners around the country, they were full of talk about half and full marathons, but very few seemed interested in running any further than 42.2 kilometres.

Perhaps it was that 'apartness' of ultra running that attracted me in the first place but, whatever it was, I found the mental and physical challenges totally absorbing. The most famous ultra at that time was the Westfield Sydney to Melbourne race (nine hundred and sixty kilometres) that brought to fame people like Cliff Young (the ultimate OFR), Yannis Kouros (probably the greatest ultra runner the world has ever seen) and another local favourite, Joe Record. I was certainly never of the calibre required to enter such a race, but I was enthralled by the concept.

What discipline did it take and where did the courage come from to suffer so greatly and get through such pain? Plus, of course, how do you train for an event that takes several days to complete, running continuously night and day along roads packed with cars, trucks and buses? More especially, it made me wonder what my own body was capable of. As I shuffled through even more 42.2-kilometre marathons, the idea of running further put its hooks into me.

I chatted to a fellow Sydney Strider, Brian Coldwell, about doing something a bit more radical and said that I had heard about an annual fifty-mile (eighty-four-kilometre) road race from Wollongong to Sydney. It played on my mind for quite a while and, probably more from bravado than common sense, I somehow found myself a formal entry in the 1983 event. Brian and I had, by then, run many marathons together and he very generously, along with another mate, offered to be my crew. Little did he, or indeed I, know what was to be involved.

Being my introduction to an ultra marathon, I'd got no idea what to expect, so the night before the race was a traumatic one, to say the least. Brian put me up for the night at his house in Clovelly, a southern coastal suburb of Sydney, but I spent most of it tossing and turning with 'what if' thoughts racing around my cartwheeling mind. Later in life, I have come to realise that this is the way I am before every event. So now I try to just let it happen and do my best to relax with some meditation, but at that time I was subject to all manner of thoughts and worries.

I was relieved when the alarm went off before four a.m. and we could head off to Wollongong for the early-morning race start. I couldn't eat a thing; my stomach was churning with nerves. The drive down there seemed endless and I was again engulfed by fear. It seemed so much longer than fifty miles. The distance itself was bad enough but what about the hills? They were extreme. Longer and steeper than anything I had experienced before and, coming shortly after the start of the race, I was sure that they would destroy me on what was forecast to be a very hot day indeed.

The promised cloudless and warm morning greeted us at the start line outside the Wollongong Town Hall at seven a.m., where a small crowd of what looked to be lean, mean and elite runners waited patiently for the gun to fire. I felt that I was the only average shuffler there, which sent even more fear surging through my body. This had the benefit of clearing my bowels out pretty well (several times, in fact) so that I was feeling as light and as ready as I would ever be.

Sure enough, by the time I had got into my stride (better recognised as a shuffle), we had reached the steep, steep hills leading out of the city. They went on for kilometre after kilometre and, just when I thought I had reached the crest of one, there was another bastard to grind me down. By then, I'm sure that I had gravel rash on my nose, the inclines were so steep. My crew kindly stopped every couple of kilometres to provide me with something to eat and drink. The ubiquitous Coca-Cola, Mars bars and jellybeans were probably not the best nutrition, but I had little to compare it to and had hardly any idea about what my body needed in such a long and difficult event.

Hour followed hour, as I struggled through high temperatures northwards along the crowded and noisy Pacific Highway towards the Sydney Town Hall. With my stride feeling to be in a wonderfully calm rhythm, I eventually crossed Tom Ugly's Bridge, which spans George's River south of Sydney. I was feeling mentally stronger since the energy-sapping hills were behind me, but I remained respectful of the distance ahead as the heat increased towards noon. I was far behind the eventual winner but was satisfied that I was doing my best. I couldn't ask for more than that.

With every step, I could feel the finish line getting closer. Drivers were sounding their car horns in encouragement and, I have to admit, I felt proud to be out there running this event, which was sadly doomed to be closed by the police the next year.

Brian joined me on the road for the last section and ultimately accompanied me across the finish line outside the Sydney Town Hall in eight hours and change, to be cheered by a small crowd of spectators and earlier finishers. I will always hold this race close to my heart, as it was where I first dipped my toes into the ocean of the ultra marathon running world. Another life-changing moment.

All these years later, I still have the T-shirt from that race and, remarkably, it still fits me. Secretly, I wear it occasionally when no one else will see me, just to bring back the special memories of a landmark day.

4

Diving Into the World of Ultras

'Running. If there is any activity happier, more exhilarating, more nourishing to the imagination, I can't think what it might be.' – Joyce Carol Oates

If there's a connection between marathons and ultra marathons, it's purely the act of running. Everything else is unconnected. When I run a marathon, I am constantly aware of the unforgiving asphalt under my feet, the cityscape hemming me in and the kilometre markers along the course. In turn, this makes me glance at my watch and think about my pace and the effect it'll have on my finishing time.

There are often crowds on the course shouting encouragement to people we don't know. We're never going to get lost and won't need to run at night, so won't require a head torch. And, heaven forbid, we wouldn't dare be seen walking a hill in the middle of a race.

But a trail ultra looks and feels very different. They take place in rugged hills or alongside raging rivers or on trails through national parks. It is the place that draws us as much as the distance.

There is usually a pre-race briefing to provide course directions. Even though it's possible to get lost, there are not too many markers out there and none of us back-of-the-packers are worried about our splits. We're all going just as fast as we can but, with so far to go, we don't fuss about a couple of minutes in an aid station. We can even take the time to sit down for a few minutes to give our legs some respite. In the night, we find someone to share the trail with and get pleasure in helping them as much as they help us.

Hills are put there for us to power hike up; after all, losing a few minutes will be more than made up later in the race by the energy conserved.

Remembering that in the mid-1980s there was no Internet, finding ultra marathon races was a question of hearing about them from friends or reading about them in magazines. Often, it was at ultras themselves that I found entry forms for upcoming races, left under a rock on tables at finishing lines. With such small fields, it was inevitable that we all got to know each other pretty well as we toured New South Wales and beyond, running as often as we could.

The events were low-budget, cheap to enter and certainly not as crowded as races are now. Everything, including the aid stations, was a lot more basic. That didn't make the races any less enjoyable, as we didn't know any better and the fun was just being out there, challenging ourselves alongside like-minded people. Trail races were growing in popularity but were still on the outer edge of the sport that was finding its feet.

And so it was that I ran a weird mixture of trail, road and track ultras in the late 1980s and into the early '90s. Also, I started to enjoy running adventures that I planned alone or with others. Looking back, I don't know why I chose to do those unheralded challenges; maybe it was just to be challenged by something different. But, whatever it was, I loved planning them on maps and organising everything that was required to make them successful. Oftentimes, I relied on local shops and cafés for nutrition along the way, but in more remote locations, I dropped food and drink off the weekend before in hidden caches. These worked well until I couldn't remember quite where I had left some of them.

One such run was in 1990 when a group of four of us Sydney Striders ran from Palm Beach, the most northerly beach, to Cronulla, the southernmost beach of greater Sydney. It must have been somewhere in the region of seventy or eighty kilometres. We did it in the height of summer, dipping our feet in the ocean at both the start and finish. It was a fun but long day out, dodging the main roads where possible. The details of the day remain a bit of a blur in my memory, apart from the four of us having to jump-start a car for someone by pushing it up a hill. It's funny how such unusual things stick in the mind over the years.

Everything just shuffled along reasonably well in those days with my life revolving around my running. I didn't have any real friends outside of that world. Sure I had acquaintances, but I didn't seem to share anything in common with them. I was certainly not interested in talking about work or what car to buy next. I became somewhat put off by the need of so many people to acquire 'things' and to live a suburban life which, in reality, I found stifling. I guess also that being an introvert by nature meant that running by myself grew more and more essential to my mental well-being. While running, I was content with who I was and didn't need to pretend that I belonged to the competitive society around me.

It was not until I read Doctor George Sheehan's wonderful book *Running and Being* that I was to fully understand that this was not something lacking in me, but rather that I was being exactly what I was meant to be, who I really was. His theory might be a generalisation of course, but I most certainly feel that he was right in my case. As an ectomorph (thin and small-boned), I could see myself in some of the things he lists as specific characteristics: 'detached, ambivalent, reticent, suspicious, cautious, awkward and reflective'. Doctor Sheehan made me realise how powerful the connection is between the physical and the mental sides of our complex being and helped me understand that there was nothing wrong with me, or my general outlook on life.

Funnily enough, I once met George Sheehan; I even ran a few kilometres with him. It was a glorious crisp Sydney spring morning and somehow he happened to join our Sydney Striders group. I was very fortunate to be able to chat to him briefly about his writing and now, as an OFR, when I read his deeply considered words, I can still hear his broad New York accent. All these years later, when looking through *Running and Being* again, I can see how right he was when he claimed that it was our body shape that determined exactly the person we would become.

In my family life as it was then, I just went through the motions, half-heartedly trying to be someone that I wasn't; to fit into a world that I was not meant to be in. I certainly loved my two kids, Stephen and Victoria, very much and used to have a lot of fun with them as they were growing up but I could see I was a social misfit. I don't think that I was ever intended to live in a world that focused on shopping centres, expensive cars and prestigious houses. I would often be asked at social functions what suburb I lived in, what school my children attended and what car I drove. I delighted in telling a few porkies just to needle my interrogators.

So it was that a running lifestyle grew within me. By lifestyle, I guess I mean that not only was it an essential part of my being, but that I was very conscious of how other parts of my life would affect my running. Things such as eating and drinking well and making sure that I got to bed early so that I was ready for a decent morning run. Perhaps others saw me as different, but I could only be true to myself, although I did try to retain a low profile.

On Sunday 11 August 1991, however, I really went off the rails. The annual fourteen-kilometre City to Surf had, by then, become the most popular running event in Sydney and possibly Australia. I had run it a few times but it had become wall-to-wall people all the way and I didn't enjoy it much any more. So I decided to do it differently that year by running the course four times, backward and forwards, before doing the organised event itself, making a total journey of seventy kilometres. To ensure that I was back in the city centre by the start of the actual race, I set out at shortly after midnight from the Sydney Town Hall. It was just an adventure with no time constraints other than being back in time for the real race to start. For the first couple of hours, it was pretty chilly and, well wrapped up, I was shuffling through crowds of drunken Saturday-night revellers who were leaving pubs or clubs as I headed out of the city.

The first challenge for me was 'Heartbreak Hill' – a long meandering hill that in the City to Surf itself has claimed many a failed PB. The first time I ran the hill, I took it fairly easy, knowing that I would be doing it a few more times. I picked up water bottles (this was early days before the sale of bottled water) that I had left out the day before, or located water bubblers in parks that I ran past. I had little to eat along the way but I did manage to find an all-night café in Bondi, near the world-famous beach race finish (and my turn-round point), that had a great brew of coffee on hand as well as toasted cheese sandwiches. I paused there twice in the night to refuel and had fun talking to the owner, who initially looked at me very strangely. I'm sure he thought that I had escaped from an asylum.

As I ran back to the city on my last leg (but certainly not my last legs), the volunteer crews were setting up aid stations along the route ready for the upcoming madness that was (and is even more so today) the City to Surf, where bands would play on the roofs of the pubs and huge cheering crowds gather along the course. There are always garden parties in full swing, champagne corks popping, as a wide variety of runners go past with the sole thought of getting to Bondi Beach and the finish.

I finally finished my quadruple prelude and arrived back at the Botanical Gardens, where I had left some clean running clothes, food and drink under a bush. I rested on a bench for a while, although I knew I wouldn't recover enough to be able to push myself hard in the main event. Since I had to hang around for more than an hour before the start of the official day's race, I was feeling quite stiff, sore and not a little hazy from the lack of sleep. So I was not fully appreciative of all that was going on around me. But I pulled myself together enough to find a spot midway in the crowd of runners. After the official start, when I was moving a bit like Tin Man from *The Wizard of Oz*, I was happy to chat to whoever chanced to be alongside me.

The last few hills of that final run were absolute torture, but I managed to finish the fourteen-kilometre race in a not too dusty sixty-five minutes. In reality, though, my time was irrelevant. I was able to smile knowing I had done what I set out to do, and that is all I could have asked. A happy man went home for a long sleep after a cooling dip and a brief rest on Bondi beach.

During this period, I continued to run the occasional marathon as well, but mostly treated them as training runs and the chance for a social catch up with my mates. My true focus was now on *ultra* marathons. They clearly required a greater commitment and definitely a greater need for obsessive behaviour – so they were a perfect fit for me.

I know that a lot of runners are focused on the Marathon Majors – big city races in New York, London, Boston, Chicago, Berlin and Tokyo. I appreciate that they can be exciting and worthwhile goals to achieve but they are not my cup of tea. For a start, I find the crowded starting pens (or corrals), where thousands of runners are squeezed in for a couple of hours before the gun goes off, to be claustrophobic and somehow in contradiction to what running is meant to symbolize; freedom and solitude. In a recent New York marathon more than forty-five thousand people waited for hours in the freezing cold. And even when the gun sent the leaders on their way, it was a long while before the ordinary runners crossed the line. After shuffling along for ages, hemmed in by the crowd, they could only get enough elbowroom to run properly after a few kilometres.

Even in the world of ultra marathons there has been a mighty explosion in the number of runners looking for a challenge. The more popular races quite often sell out in minutes and some of the more famous ultras have even introduced a lottery system because they are totally swamped with applications. So the entry fees have escalated, but that hasn't stopped the start lines from being jam-packed with all levels of athletes.

Not for me, though, thank you very much – give me the small town marathons or ultras every time. They are cheaper to enter, you can park not far away, there's no queue at the Portaloos and you only need to arrive shortly before the start. To top it all off, you will probably know a few of the other runners. As they say, small is beautiful and the way to go.

5

Pushing My Limits

'The secret of the greatest fruitfulness and the greatest enjoyment of existence is to live dangerously.' – Friedrich Nietzsche

As the years passed, I pursued my running with a passion and entered as many races as my body would allow. Race after race filled my calendar. I ran in Hong Kong, Canberra, Melbourne, country Victoria and throughout New South Wales. There were beginning to be just as many races on trails as there were on roads. I was attracted to them one and all.

    I developed the habit of running once a week from my home in the north-western suburbs of Sydney into the CBD, where I worked (a hilly trek of about thirty-five kilometres) thereby gladly squeezing in a second long run. The traffic along the main highway was so heavy that sometimes it seemed that I reached the CBD faster on foot. Mind you, I avoided the main roads wherever I could, even if it meant having to run further. These runs, of course, meant leaving home early, usually in the dark. I didn't have time to eat before leaving but I was always able to find taps or hoses in people's front gardens to scrounge a drink from. I used to look forward to buying a large coffee and some raisin toast when I eventually arrived in town, before showering and heading to work.

    Occasionally, on a warm summer day, I would drive to a harbourside suburb in the early morning and, with a backpack holding a change of clothes, run into the city. These runs were along wonderful bush trails which, now and then, would emerge into a small, exclusive enclave of houses before diving back into stands of gum trees. The bush resonated with the trilling sound of cicadas and the raucous calls of sulphur-crested cockatoos high in the canopy. On those days, I would change back into my smelly running gear, leave the office after work and shuffle back the way I had come, albeit a little slower and stiffer.

In 1987, however, my world changed irrevocably. Two years before the Global Financial Crisis, a radical amendment to government legislation caused my job to become redundant. In losing a well-paid position, I also became separated from my first wife. Sadly, in the years leading up to that point, we had both become very different people to those we had been when we met as teenagers.

As things deteriorated, it became clear that our marriage was at an end. I felt terrible for our children, Stephen and Victoria, especially as I would only see them every other weekend. Even though we regularly spoke on the phone and had fun when we were together, it never really made up for the gap that grew between us. I am fortunate that, despite those difficulties, we are close today.

After a year or so of working at makeshift jobs, I was finally able to land a position with Prudential Insurance Company in their Sydney office. To get even that job in such a terrible economic climate was hard, so I felt quite lucky to be in at least a financially secure position.

The job may have been mundane and uninspiring but, once again, I fell on my feet running-wise. Throughout the various levels of the organisation there were runners of every kind, shape and size – but they all had one thing in common. They loved running and what it did for them. I quickly melded into the workplace and the running scene.

We were fortunate to have a change room with a shower, so lunchtime outings were common. We soon formed a Corporate Cup team and on Wednesdays, fortnightly, we raced around the six-kilometre course in the Sydney Botanical Gardens. We never won anything and, as far as I can recall, we were usually towards the bottom of the ladder, but it was good to have a timed event that became an integral part of my training.

It was while working at Prudential during my marriage break-up, when I was finding it extraordinarily hard to cope with all that seemed to be heaping up around me, that I turned inward even more than before. I closed the world out as best I could. My sole saviour was running.

Several days a week I arrived at the office around seven thirty a.m. and worked hard until five or six p.m. I would then be like Clark Kent, becoming a different person with a swift change of clothes. Carrying a small backpack, containing some water and a couple of bananas, I would head off from the city on an unplanned adventure evening. For long hours in the dark, I shuffled through a wide variety of Sydney suburbs, some of which I had never heard of. I bought food and more water along the way from late-night milk bars whose owners eyed me suspiciously. Dressed in skimpy gear, sweating profusely and looking a little otherworldly in the middle of the night, who could blame them?

Years later, reading Dean Karnazes's book *Ultra Marathon Man* and the description of his first long run, the memories of my long nights flooded back to me. I met many interesting people of all nationalities who wanted to know where I had come from, where I was going and why. I shared stories with such a vast number of genuine people that, before I set off from work each evening, I was excited about what would happen along the way.

Over the three years that I did this, I never once had to deal with a difficult or unpleasant situation. Although I was running alone and in what were regarded as dangerous areas, I always felt safe. Even in the red-light district of Kings Cross, drunks and ladies of the night would shout out to me and we would exchange a few cheerful words before I pushed on. Now, as an OFR, I don't think I would feel so much at ease in such places.

Those unplanned adventures would take several hours and sometimes I wouldn't reach home until after midnight, exhausted but with my mind happily emptied of all thoughts about my life. At that stage, all I cared about was sleep and getting ready for the next day to do it all over again. Maybe this obsessive running away from the things that were happening to me was bad, but those night runs certainly toughened me up. I was primed to run anything I wanted to at the drop of a hat – and I did. It did not matter if it was an organised event or just an unscheduled adventure outing.

Sometimes on a weekend, I would catch a train to an outlying Sydney station and shuffle home, taking whichever road seemed to be in the right direction – avoiding as best I could the busy major traffic arteries. Only once or twice did I have any company, but I really enjoyed the solitude and the mindlessness of those long hours. Things haven't changed much over the years. As an OFR, the solitude is still one of the reasons I love my running so much.

All this long-distance stuff changed me, both physically and mentally. I am sure that it made me even more closed off from the world than before. Most noticeable of all was the radical change in my body. I gave more thought to what I was eating and drinking, becoming a vegetarian, losing a few kilos that further added to my mean, lean appearance. In retrospect, I can see that it was further evidence of my obsessive-compulsive nature at work. My running style had evolved into an economical 'ultra shuffle', with shorter strides, a faster tempo and feet barely lifting of the ground. It was clear, even to me, things were getting a little extreme and starting to take their toll. I came down with far too many colds and minor injuries, which had a cumulative effect, and ultimately I had to pay the price for overdoing things.

Looking back on those days and nights of crazy running, I am certainly not proud of the way I used running to hide from the world and wish that I had shown more fortitude in the face of adversity. Unfortunately, however, that is water under the bridge. I can't change what happened, but I now know better and try to keep my life well balanced. Mind you, I don't always succeed.

At the end of 1991, things came to a head. I had just finished a gruelling twenty-four-hour track race where I felt comfortable for the first twenty-three hours but pushed too hard for the last hour and did huge damage to a groin muscle. Rather than rest, I assumed that the pain would go away by itself and so I kept up my obsessive and manic training schedule. The price I paid was high – the injury got worse and worse; every step hurt every day. I had no alternative but to stop altogether.

Being forced to stop doing what is central to your being is difficult to describe. Later, I talk about how, in my seventies, I am fighting what again feels like an almost annihilation of self, but back in 1991 my destruction felt complete and irreversible. Of course, as time passed, I kept lacing up my shoes and heading out the door for a run, only to be brought to a halt quickly with returning pain from that historic injury. I was forced to walk home feeling shattered and frustrated every time.

I found that the only way to come to terms with the anguish that seemed to ooze from every pore was to try and block running from my mind altogether. I pursued the usual alternatives of cycling and swimming but, after giving them a fair chance, they didn't do the trick. Since my second wife, Dale, liked to go to the gym, I went along with her and tried to keep fit through a regular exercise programme. Unlike running, I found the gym hard work and even a little claustrophobic – but gradually I started to enjoy the endorphins from a hard workout, so I persevered.

I didn't know if I was ever going to be able to run properly again and couldn't even think about such a possibility. I just wanted to stay in some sort of shape and get the most out of life. One day at a time.

The best thing to come out of my years of working at Prudential was that I met Dale. She was my boss for a while, which made it a bit tricky at times, but it was worth the effort and we have spent twenty-five almost idyllic years together; many of those years have been on Flinders Island in the Roaring Forties down in Tasmania. We are now totally incapable of living on the Australian mainland; life couldn't get any better than it is here.

6

Running For Charity

'You have to go looking for happiness in life, but find it in the things that make you feel alive. Life is not something to be pressured and protected. It is to be explored and lived to the full.'
– Killian Jornet (perhaps the greatest trail and mountain ultra runner of all time)

Daylight cranks up and the clouds start to lift from the offshore islands in the Franklin Sound we can see from our bed. My wife and I sit there entranced by the shifts in light and the ever-changing view, sipping our first cup of coffee, deciding what the weather is going to give us and what choices the day will provide. But one thing is certain – I will go for a good run first thing. After the dog has been fed, of course.

There is no other choice for me; I prefer to run on an empty stomach and I much prefer to get my run in before anything else happens. Far too often, the daily demands of life can get in the way and it is too easy to find a reason *not* to lace up my shoes if I delay the decision. Chores like working in the vegie garden, mowing or splitting wood can wait until my mind-clearing hour's encounter with my inner self has been fulfilled.

It is, of course, a personal choice. Quite a few runners I know prefer to get out on the roads or trails after work – but I'm firmly of the belief that running early sets me up for the day ahead both physically and mentally. Maybe it's like pressing the reset button every morning; I am always more positive and definitely more creative after I've run. I feel like I have more energy for all that life can throw at me. Like so many other runners,

I find that life's tensions fade away and my sense of self-worth improves. Who needs a psychiatrist when you own a pair of running shoes?

Somehow, the weather feels more suited to running in the mornings too. In the summer months, it still feels cool and refreshing (at least here in Tasmania) while the sun is low in the sky. The towering gum trees are still redolent of eucalyptus oil and the eternal breaking of ocean waves seems to make the world sound more peaceful. It can be a bit of a sensory overload and sometimes I find it hard to turn round and head for home.

Of course, winter is a different story. Here on Flinders Island, we get all kinds of weather, apart from snow. At that time of year, we have chilly mornings with strong winds, often accompanied by squally rain. The best way to tackle this is to not even think about it. Jump out of bed, throw on a few layers of gear, grab a quick coffee and do it. If I were an afternoon runner, I would have all day to think about the conditions I would face, and find it very easy to chicken out. A two- or three-hour run in miserable weather may sound unattractive to start with, but if you just put one foot in front of the other, focus on positive things such as your goals or the reason for running in the first place, you will soon find yourself at the halfway mark and feeling pleased that you are doing it.

Somewhere in the Bible it tells us that there is a time for every purpose – and my time for running is first thing in the morning on an empty stomach alongside a happy dog, before anything can interfere with it.

Occasionally, I will also head out for a second run in the evening with our local running group but I treat that as purely a social outing; a time to meet other like-minded people, talk running trash and enjoy a cold beer and a barbecue afterwards. And I have to admit you can't do that first thing in the morning.

To get back into running again in 2004 following my forced hiatus took a huge effort. After we moved to Flinders Island, our twenty-five-year old daughter Allison was diagnosed with a virulent form of cancer. She fought it strongly and in between chemotherapy sessions she always went running in her local park, swam and attended regular yoga classes. Her strength and determination were so inspiring to our family and all her friends.

After three years, despite aggressive surgery and a huge fighting spirit, Allison sadly lost her battle and the family was left completely shell-shocked. We obviously supported each other through this time of grief, but I felt the need to find solitude and looked again to running as my way of coping with such deep sadness. It had been over ten years since I was able to run at all, so I was delighted to find that I could run/walk down our isolated bush trails and feel the recuperative power of nature doing its work.

At nearly sixty years of age, it felt strange, though; my body resisted all the extra effort, but in my head there was a reconnection with those earlier years. I was finally resurfacing as a runner. Having returned to the bottom of the exercise ladder with my soft untrained body, I knew that the comeback trail wasn't going to be easy.

The long process involved much walking at the start, but gradually I was able to increase the running periods, as long as I allowed for recovery breaks. It was grand to again feel that cycle of work, pain and recovery. I was quick to feel the benefits mentally as well and started to get excited about being good enough to enter a race or two.

Whenever we travelled off the island, I started to search out events that could be like stepping stones in the measurement of my ability. Eventually, I progressed, much as I had done before, through half marathons up to a full marathon. Once I had that under my belt, I began to feel indestructible again – but this time, I told myself it would be different. I assured myself that I would listen to my ageing body and take better care of it than I had previously. The bottom line was, however, that I knew I was once again a runner, was always meant to be a runner and would never be anything else. It felt wonderful and I wanted it to stay that way.

The terrible loss of Allison remained fresh in our family's minds. We felt it wasn't enough to mourn her loss but rather that we should find ways to help those organisations devoted to finding a cure for cancer. My wife Dale and I found that Cure Cancer Australia was seeking donations to help young researchers come up with new ideas to rid society of cancer in the long term, so we got their permission to raise funds on their behalf.

We started off by holding a second-hand bookstall at our island's quarterly market. When we had moved to Flinders Island, we had taken roughly ten thousand books with us but we couldn't hope to fit them all into our small home. The local market was an ideal place to offload a large quantity and benefit a charity. As time went on, however, the locals kept donating their excess books and so we continued to hold the stall for a number of years, raising substantial amounts for Cure Cancer Australia.

It was in 2011 when I was sixty-four and a confirmed OFR that my love of long-distance running was reaching its second peak (or should I say crescendo?) and everything changed for me. I felt ready to step up to a fund-raising challenge that would test my limits and appeal to the generosity of our small island community, numbering little more than eight hundred at that time. When I examined the map of Flinders Island, I discovered that the main north/south road was measured at seventy-six kilometres. Somehow, running the entire length of the island fired my imagination. Something that has never been done before is always appealing and I thought that it would be a great opportunity to raise more funds for Cure Cancer Australia.

Immediately, I received tremendous support from our caring islanders. Businesses as well as kind individuals donated many items for me to auction at a fund-raising dinner held before the event and people were happy to pay five dollars a guess to win a donated return air ticket to Launceston for being the closest to my overall run time. Dale (who helped tremendously in this fund-raising effort) and I proudly raised a total of ten thousand dollars.

This was all very inspiring, but now I had to pay the price by running the distance. I upped my training mileage, spending the most time simulating the upcoming run on gravel roads, becoming more and more obsessive in planning every detail of the adventure. I knew that it would push me to my limits but I was not going to back down, even when training meant getting out the door for a long run on wild, wild winter mornings wrapped up heavily against the icy cold wind and rain.

The charity run, which I named the Big Run 4A Cure, took place on 30 October 2011 in the middle of our spring. I was starting at the northernmost point of the island, in a small holiday village called Palana, with a happy group of local runners who so very generously wanted to support the whole run. It turned out to be a dreadful pre-run night in the shack where we were staying. After the ubiquitous pasta dinner, a violent storm sent solid sheets of rain drumming down on the tin roof, while the worst westerly wind shook the building to within an inch of its life. I was sharing a room with a young runner, David Green, and neither of us got much sleep that night as we nervously thought about what lay ahead of us the next morning. I was more on edge than the other David, who knew he would only be running shorter legs and have the chance to get warm in between.

As expected, it turned out to be a miserable day weather-wise, with chilly headwinds all the way and some showers just to keep us honest. The first half of the run was on gravel roads which, at that time of year, were quite corrugated and difficult to get a rhythm on, but things got easier once we hit the paved road halfway to the Lady Barron township at the south-eastern end of the island. What made the run especially memorable was the group of local runners and walkers who joined me in many places along the way. The local postman, John Clifford, allowed me to slipstream him for a long time and a local running legend, Brown Dog, ran with his master Mike Withers for about the half the day. David Green made several appearances and even my friend Spud Murphy, who is not a long-distance runner, turned out and covered about twenty kilometres with me.

Without them all, it would have been much harder and certainly a lot less fun. Many locals came out to cheer us all on as well as making on-the-spot donations to boost our kitty. It took me nine and a bit hours for this north to south run but my body held up very well through all the adversity that the weather gods threw at us. Towards the end of the day, my quads felt the effect of the downhills but I was able to push myself for a fast finish to the Lady Barron Wharf. It's amazing what the body can do.

I found it hard to change from being purely a social runner, one who likes being under the radar just entering events that attract me, to being in the spotlight, using what I did for fun to also be a vehicle for fund-raising. Having to make speeches and be interviewed on the radio took a lot of practice before it became even a little more natural. I would much sooner have remained anonymous and I felt a bit embarrassed when people said such things as 'I don't know how you do it' or 'you're such an inspiration'. It was purely something that I wanted to do to challenge myself and to benefit a worthwhile charity.

Several years later, to celebrate my seventieth birthday, I thought that it would be a good idea to see how long it would take to run the length of the island in the opposite direction, from south to north. Why such a thought came to me I can't explain; I must have been feeling a bit bored or drunk too much bad wine. So it was that in May 2017, again joined by many locals, including the ever-present Brown Dog, I headed out from the southernmost port of Lady Barron towards my ultimate goal of Palana, in the north.

Of course the weather hadn't changed one bit; windy and wet all day with occasional heavy dumps of rain that certainly slowed us up. A generous friend, Helen Haines, had a huge vat of soup ready for all of us at the halfway mark, inside one of the island's small fire stations. These are moments that always mean so much. The sense of achievement is multiplied when others give up their time to be involved in making a project successful. As well as a good number of local runners supporting me, I had a couple of ultra mates, Lib Smith and Gerry Santamaria, fly over to enjoy the day with me. It was a wonderful community spirit.

In between those island runs, in 2015, I put together a two-hundred-kilometre run from Launceston to Hobart to raise as much money for Cure Cancer Australia as I could. The plan was to run forty kilometres a day for five days. I called the run 200kms 4a Cure and went out looking for sponsorship. This is always a difficult challenge, as so much is asked of organisations these days. I was keen to make sure that any support I was given received as much exposure as possible in return.

It started very well, with our local airline, Sharp Airlines, donating two return tickets to Launceston, which was followed by cash donations from Bendigo (and Rural) Bank, Nichols Poultry and the financial planning organisation Godfrey Pembroke (who also put on a cocktail evening in their Launceston offices the night before the run started). Other help came from our Flinders Council and a couple of solid financial businesses. With such generous support, I could afford to hire a small campervan for the volunteer crew as well as all our gear and we proudly stuck the sponsors' eye-catching logos all over it.

In the latter stages of getting everything set up, a new running friend, Scott Jones, came into the mix by offering to run the whole distance with me. This was certainly unexpected and I was very excited at the thought of having some company along the way. However, it developed beyond that, as Scotty had a large family and many friends who lived along the route and, therefore, he was able to bring a large support network into the mix. As it turned out, this made a huge difference to both the enjoyment and success of the run itself. Several Launceston runners who knew Scotty but had never met me also turned out to run a lot of kilometres on the first two days, as well as joining in the final trot into Hobart.

I had been having some issues with the adductor muscle in my left leg. Worried that it would impact badly on my running on roads for those five days, I was forced to take the whole week off from running before the event. Even so, some discomfort remained and I felt uneasy about it all until we started. Amazingly, it was forgotten when I was running. It was only when we rested each evening that the tightness returned. I got into the habit of stretching the sore area and that seemed to help. But overall my body survived pretty well, which I put down to doing my long-distance training runs mostly on the softer trails at home.

As seems standard for all my charity runs, the weather for 200kms 4a Cure was unpredictable, with a lot of fast-moving dark clouds occasionally dumping heavy downpours on us, but we remained in good spirits as the kilometres clicked over. Our lunch breaks were planned to be in villages along the Midland Highway (the main road between Launceston and Hobart) that gave a chance for runners to catch up with our campervan crew, consisting mainly of my wife Dale and the amazing family of Scotty Jones. One unforgettable lunch stop was in a tiny village called Bagdad (different spelling; different place, thank goodness), where we sat outside a small café/ petrol station, rapidly consuming a batch of egg rolls, plus bacon for the meat-eaters, washed down with steaming cups of coffee. As happens on such runs, this meal was a talking point for miles both before in anticipation and afterwards with satisfaction.

Every now and then, much to our delight, one of the support crew would jump out of the bus in running gear and shuffle along with us for a while. Jo Youl, a lively and well built young island woman, was in our crew for a couple of days and got to thinking 'if that Old Fart can do it, so can I' – so she jumped out of the bus in a pair of black Skins and a tight T-shirt. Feeling pretty sparky, she started to race up the road ahead of Scotty and me. Embarrassingly for her, there was a large male crew working on some road improvements and, seeing Jo in her skimpy, tight gear, they gave her raucous encouragement. Scotty and I were happily shuffling along some way behind but we could hear the whistles and good-humoured racket ahead of us. By the time we got to the same spot, the hi-vis-clad workers told us we'd have to get a wriggle on if we were to catch her and that 'she's a better-looking runner than you blokes are'.

We had plenty of people from some amazingly diverse backgrounds join in and run at different times, including one of our major sponsors,

Dane Waldron from Godfrey Pembroke. Now, Dane hadn't run at all for many years but he pulled out all the stops and covered nearly twenty kilometres, including some pretty gnarly hills. Dane just loves a good cause. We even had the Tasmanian Liberal Party member Michael Ferguson come and run with us for a while. It goes to show that some politicians can get it right; and it wasn't even an election year.

Overnight on that adventure we stayed in motels or pubs close to the highway and were able to eat hearty meals together and get plenty of good rest. It was lovely to laugh and talk over the events of the day, helping bond our little group even further. To be honest, doing a multi-day run is a lot easier on this ageing body, which increasingly needs to have somewhat greater recovery than in my younger days.

After the first couple of days, I got into a wonderful rhythm with my running and it all felt very easy. When it was time to stop for the night, I always felt reasonably fresh and was keen to keep going. But we had arranged to meet different groups at certain points along the way so we had to make sure the timing was spot on. This feeling of strength in my not so young body was interesting and would help me make decisions in the future about what I was capable of achieving. People have often told me that I should be taking things more easily, but my experience up to that time had shown that I was capable of achieving whatever goals I set for myself. I may have been slower but I would get there in the end.

I was very proud to be joined on the final day by two of our daughters, Heather and Vicki, who had flown in from Tamworth and Sydney, plus quite a few local people who had heard about the fund-raising run. I think about twelve of us ran the last section into Hobart; that made it really special.

We were welcomed into Hobart by the Lord Mayor, Damon Thomas, and at the finish line Kristie Williams, a young lady from one of the sponsors, Bendigo Bank, presented me with a substantial cheque for donations she had personally raised. Sometimes, words can't say what I feel but if you ever read this, Kristie, I have to tell you once again how moved I was by your support, especially as you ran with us on that fabulous last day.

My main recollection of the finish is of everyone involved sitting in sunshine (yes, it finally came out at the end of the run) outside a pub on the Hobart wharf enjoying some ice-cold beers and a large lunch. The feeling I had was one of tremendous pride, not just in my achievement but also in having such caring people share it with me, helping to raise a substantial sum of money for Cure Cancer research. All the preparation had paid off.

Obviously, fund-raising for Cure Cancer was the central objective of this run and I was just blown away by the response from the ordinary people who gave us donations along the way. Occasionally, a car would pull over and some dollar notes were thrust into our hands with the comment that they too had had cancer touch their family and wanted to help in the fight to find a cure. But the one person who stands out in my mind was an older, poorly dressed woman who looked like a homeless person. She could barely walk across the road in a pair of broken sandals, but insisted on giving me five dollars towards our cause. What was clearly a generous contribution from her purse moved me greatly and helped keep me motivated at a tough time in the day. Sometimes, there are people who touch your life so very briefly but make a big impact in one way or another; this was definitely such a person.

The power of running for charitable fund-raising is, of course, nothing new and it had been highlighted for me a couple of years earlier by the great ultra runner Pat Farmer. Our island holds a running festival over the first weekend of September each year and we invite a keynote speaker for our pasta night before the big race, which is a twenty-six-kilometre pub-to-pub event. We have had such great Australian athletes as Steve Moneghetti, Hanny Allston, Sam Gash, Nova Peris and Debbie De Williams (who ran around Australia), but one year we invited Pat Farmer to come down and join in. We were excited when he accepted our invitation and were able to attract a full house to the pre-race dinner that evening.

Well, not only did Pat give us a truly inspirational talk about his mammoth fund-raising runs around the world (including the famed Pole to Pole run), but he also joined in the running events over the weekend and then refused to accept the fee that we had agreed to pay him for his work. This is a man who makes his living from such presentations and undertakes humungous charity fund-raising efforts, so we were quite taken aback by his generosity.

On top of that, he offered to be the ambassador of our event and do what he could to encourage others to come down to Flinders Island to take part in future running festivals. Listening to Pat's presentation affirmed my desire to continue to raise funds for Cure Cancer and that running should always be an adventure that aims to benefit as many people as possible.

He also reminded me that, despite ageing bodies, we are all capable of achieving a lot more than we would think. He is a prime example of setting big, hairy-arsed goals that we should all learn from. All we have to do is prepare, commit and achieve. Those three verbs are instilled in me as being critical for success in any venture, whether it be a running one or not.

Where to from here, I wondered after completing the run to Hobart? I was an Old Fart Runner with a renewed running problem; once again, I found that as soon as one event had finished I needed another fix and, if I didn't find a good one quickly, the 'blue funk' would come over me. Just going for a jog every day was wonderful but to fuel my passion I desperately needed to discover new challenges, ideally in strange, remote and wild places; places where solitude would work its wonders on me.

7

Heading to the Desert

'Dream of things that never were and ask why not.' – George Bernard Shaw

Time does strange and wonderful things to us. I particularly feel this as I age. I don't want to waste time but rather grab life with both hands and suck the marrow out of it, as Henry David Thoreau once wrote. Sure, it is sometimes difficult to free ourselves up to make decisions to do things that may seem crazy at the time, but this is the only life we're going to have, so it's crazy that we should live it unfulfilled.

The opportunities coming my way as an OFR are shrinking day by day. I know that I am now incapable of a sub-twenty-four-hour hundred-miler or qualifying for any one of many great tests of human endurance that have harsh cut-off times. But this doesn't mean that I have to stop challenging myself. In my senior years, I want to remain a runner, doing things outside of the restrictive square box.

Back in 2015, I had been recovering from my fund-raising runs. I was sixty-eight and, as usual after such an uplifting time, was feeling somehow empty. After months of training and focusing on my charity events, that emptiness hung heavily on me. Without reaching out for the next adventure, it was natural to feel lost and flat.

I was driving Dale crazy, and urgently needed to find something to lift myself out of it. In a running magazine, I came across a large, brightly coloured advertisement for a multi-day desert race that looked like it would fit the bill. Something about the overall challenge of the Big Red Run sounded extremely exciting, probably because it seemed beyond my ability and yet romantically appealing at the same time. Six days running in the Simpson Desert were bound to be inspiring and uplifting.

There was no doubt I had to do it, even though the cost of the whole thing looked excessive. In addition, one of the entry requirements was that I had to raise $1,000 for the charity Junior Diabetes Research Fund. One of our family members had recently been diagnosed as a sufferer of type 1 diabetes, so there was an added incentive to help. Apart from everything else, I was sure that this event would prove to be a lot of fun and rewarding at the same time.

So it was that I had the standard running event conversation with my wife.

Me (in my most charming voice): Darling, I've just come across this amazing race on the Internet. Wow, does it sounds great? It's got my name written all over it.

Dale: Oh yes? Another one? Where is it and when is it?

Me: I've forgotten the details, but I'll check it out again. (To myself, hee, hee.)

Dale: Oh, sure. Come on, spit it out.

Me: OK, I think it's next July and it's in the Simpson Desert. Two hundred and fifty kilometres over six days.

Dale: Are you crazy or what?

Me (after a long pause): I'll be fine. I've got plenty of time to train. So, what d'you think? It would be amazing to do it. How exciting will running in the desert be?

Dale (sighing): Send me the link. I'd like to know more about it before I say anything that might incriminate me. How much is it?

Me: Just the price of an air ticket.

Dale: A ticket to where?

Me: Europe. Ha ha.

Once Dale had generously agreed to it, I registered, making a large dollar deposit, and then excitedly turned my mind to preparation. Now, as I have said before, I tend to be quite obsessive about organising things. Over the years, I have always enjoyed spending many hours getting holiday travel itineraries down pat almost as much as the actual holiday itself. If I can put everything into order, even using spreadsheets, I am happy. So it was with excitement that I plunged into planning for the Big Red Run.

A good starting point for me was the list of mandatory gear that every runner had to take to the desert. This included many items that I had purchased for earlier races, but I discovered that I also needed to spend quite large sums on a sleeping bag, inflatable mattress, down jacket and other essentials required to survive the run and the accompanying tent life. This was fantastic, a new way to spend a fortune – just what I needed to find fulfilment.

Such wonders as gaiters now entered onto my radar. I looked at pictures of various kinds on the Internet and marvelled at the colours and styles people put over their shoes. Did I need those that just clipped on to the upper part of the shoe, or was it necessary to ensure that the whole shoe was covered? I was flabbergasted to see they even produced knee-length versions that guaranteed not to let any sand in, but the photos looked ridiculous. One of my future tent mates, Markus Schar, had previously run the Marathon des Sables across the Sahara Desert and pointed me in the direction of a gaiter that was either stitched or glued to the shoe, covering the whole thing, and ultimately fitted tightly above the ankle.

I noticed from the mandatory gear list that I also needed a compass. Apart from worrying about the fact that this implied that I could get lost in the desert, I was also concerned about how to use a compass properly. So, of course, I had to buy a book on how to read maps and influence people.

My new Excel spreadsheet had as many columns as a Greek temple and I enjoyed spending many rest days entering every item required, the purchase date, cost, weight and anything else I could think of. The biggest issue that I needed to worry about was the food that should be taken, bearing in mind there was a pretty tight weight restriction imposed on every runner. I had never had to think about this before, so I asked for help from as many people as I could track down who had experience in multi-day racing. It became clear that freeze-dried food was the best way to approach the issue and, thank goodness again for the Internet, I was able to find quite a few websites that cater to such requirements. Another money pit discovered, oh joy of joys. The puzzle of what had been solved but the issue of *how much* weighed heavily (excuse the pun) on my mind. After all, in everyday conditions, with my metabolism, I need to eat something every couple of hours. To be able to run all day every day for six days, adequate nutrition was going to need careful consideration.

Eventually, I decided that a light breakfast of porridge with a couple of cups of strong coffee was all that I would need before each day's run, but when I finished I would want a fair amount of protein (in the form of a shake, preferably chocolate) to aid muscle recovery. I would also need a snack to nibble on during the afternoon (in the optimistic hope that I would be back at the campsite before dark each day) and then a freeze-dried meal of some sort in the evening. Being a vegetarian somewhat limited my choices but I managed to find an interesting variety and got a good supply posted to me. I quickly tested one meal but it was so bad I decided not to eat any more before I had to.

My tent mate to be, Markus, had discovered an overseas supplier of freeze-dried chocolate pudding. After building up my hopes for a bit of luxury, it was discovered that they couldn't ship to Australia, so I would have to make do with something less exotic for dessert. I stuck with bars of dark chocolate.

Of course, I would also have to eat a fair bit when I was running. In this regard, I was on safer ground as I had used and enjoyed a variety of foods in previous ultras. I like to use a wide range of gels, especially savoury ones rather than the traditional very sugary recipes that tend to get a bit much on a long run. I had found that Hammer sold a powdered nutrition drink called Perpetuem, which worked very well in practice, but when I used it in hot conditions, I found it hard to swallow. I was excited to find, however, that they produced a solid tablet version that you just chewed and was perfect for a hot desert race. The additional weight was a bit of an issue but I preferred to make sure I had enough nutrition rather than extra running clothes. I would just have to keep using the same gear day after day and stink along with everybody else.

Talking of nutrition, Markus introduced me to Nutella as a great source of carbohydrates and it soon became a favourite treat out on training runs. I was uncertain, however, about carrying it in my backpack out there in the desert heat. So I was especially pleased when I found that Hammer also produced a gel that tasted like Nutella and was handier to carry.

This was my first experience of a multi-day race so I was certainly pretty scared and, as usual, in the last few days before I caught the bus to Birdsville from Adelaide, every part of my body felt exhausted and unable to run a step. This, in turn, created a feeling of panic and despair that I wouldn't be able to finish even the first day's stage. It was a familiar feeling from previous races but, talking to the other runners on the bus, I was relieved to find that I was not alone in this regard. I felt a lot easier about it all and was able to relax a little and enjoy the scenery along the way.

The bus ride up to the start in Birdsville was fantastic and remains clear in my memory. We left from the Adelaide central bus depot at seven-thirty a.m. on a Saturday and headed north until we got to the almost deserted township of Maree, where we spent the night. It used to be an important stop on the Ghan railway but became a backwater when the line was diverted many years ago. Only a few people now live there permanently but it's an interesting place to stay overnight. We all had a good pub meal and a couple of beers before climbing the stairs for a fitful sleep (at least in my case).

After Maree, the tarmac road ended and we continued heading north up the Birdsville Track into the real Aussie outback. The road itself was rough; gravel with large loose rocks and huge potholes that made the journey seem even longer than the day it took. We got our first real sight of the desert country here and were surprised to see that it wasn't all sand. Rocks and low grey/green scrub dominated the scenery as far as the eye could see. There were no trees, no hills, just the biggest sky I'd ever seen. It was fun to stop for lunch at the iconic Mungerannie Hotel that stood slap bang in the middle of nowhere. There was no other habitation for hundreds of kilometres but somehow they had acquired a McDonald's sign that advertised 'coming soon to this location'.

The pub/motel was unique in that over the years a lot of people had nailed a part of their ponytail or a clipping of their hair to the ceiling. Names and dates were attached, while odd articles of underwear also made good conversation pieces. The landlord was one of those strange fellows who have probably lived on their own out in the bush for far too long. Mind you, it was certainly entertaining to listen to his bizarre stories.

By now, us runners were getting to know each other better, boding well for the next week or so, as we'd be returning together again on the bus after the race. We swapped stories about past races and wondered at length about running in the desert. Someone mentioned that they had heard about the gibber plains lying out in the desert waiting for us. They were said to have a terrible effect on the feet of runners. We were all scared about what we'd face but on the other hand couldn't wait to get started.

The Simpson Desert is the largest parallel dune system in the world and, from looking at the maps we had been given, it seemed that we were going to cross most of them, including the biggest daddy of them all, Big Red as it's known.

By the time the bus pulled up at the Birdsville Hotel on that Sunday afternoon, we were all in absolute awe of the location. The tarmac roads of the little township were edged with fine sand that continually drifted in from the surrounding desert. There weren't many people around but those we met in the few local shops were interested in what we were doing in town. They didn't often see such large groups and a crazy bunch of desert runners had them scratching their heads.

About fifty of us spent the first night camping in the town's sports centre. Others stayed in their tents or luxuriated in the comparative comfort of the unique Birdsville Hotel. We then had the next morning (Monday) free to explore every corner of Birdsville. Not that there are many corners, but it's an interesting little place; so remote but with everything you could want – the bakery even sold exotic camel pies, which were a great hit with many of the runners.

Being winter, the mornings were pretty chilly but soon warmed up, which didn't augur well for the race conditions in the days ahead. I didn't want to do too much the day before the race so, before registration and the mandatory gear check, I headed over to the hotel to test their adult beverage and catch some of the local atmosphere.

From there, it was over to the township's community centre for some race information sessions as well as the ubiquitous gear check. I was a little nervous about this as I understood that the organisers were very strict on the weight of the bag (fourteen kilograms) that would be transported from camp to camp for us. I had spent so many evenings at home and then on the journey to Birdsville checking and rechecking that I had everything I was meant to have. Such things always cause me to worry, as you can be eliminated from the race before it even begins if there is any mandatory gear missing, but I was fine this time. I was fairly sure that I was close to the weight limit but didn't want to have to carry any excess in my day pack which, holding the four kilograms of mandatory gear, before any water was added, I reckoned would weigh enough anyway. Fortunately I was judged to be just under the limit, so retired to our temporary home in the sports centre for a bit of a nap. This proved impossible with so many people hyped up about everything, but a quiet pre-race buffet dinner and an early night for us all set the scene for the following day.

Race morning hadn't quite dawned when we awoke and prepared ourselves for a seven-thirty a.m. race start. I managed to organise a cup of coffee and an energy bar but that was all my nerves would allow at that stage. I had packed plenty of food to eat on the run during the day, so I wasn't unduly worried.

Everyone wandered over to the inflated start line gantry directly outside the hotel, where we were each given a location tracker to put in our backpack as a safety measure. Then it was just a matter of standing around in the chilly air excitedly waiting for the start that we had all anticipated for so long. It seemed surreal that the moment had come at last.

Was I ready for the days ahead? I forced the thought out of my mind and just made mindless chatter with people who were strangers then, but whom I would know so well by the end.

8

The Gibbers Strike

'Your body will argue that there is no justifiable reason to continue. Your only recourse is to call on your spirit, which fortunately functions independently of logic.' – Tim Noakes

Ultra marathons grind you down physically and mentally, but the Big Red Run stripped me bare. Right down to the bone. We were thrown into three challenging marathons in the first three days across some pretty rugged country, including the demoralising red rock gibber plains, one after the other. I was totally demolished; a raw bag of nerves and bloody feet, sitting in a puddle of fluid left on the desert floor.

As we shuffled out of Birdsville at the start of the event to a smattering of applause, we were welcomed by vast blue skies, bright beyond any I had previously experienced. Perhaps it was too early for the dust to have blown in from the wide, empty desert spaces. The horizons were so vast, edged by dunes as far as the eye could see. As we moved deeper into the Simpson Desert, the sun rose higher and higher, getting hotter every minute.

From the first footsteps, as we ran out of the township on that crisp morning in June 2015, the extreme isolation of the run became clear. There was nothing but empty desert ahead of us. We were running off the map into a wilderness that, in my mind, was going to be littered with the skeletal remains of old explorers like Burke and Wills. All we knew was that somewhere out there, beyond the Black Stump, the organisers were setting up our first night's campsite.

The mere thought of the freedom of being in such a place as this, with limitless horizons and crystal clear air, had been with me for what seemed a lifetime and now I was here. I was going to soak it all up, store it in my memory banks and keep it close to me for the rest of my life.

I've never been renowned for my good looks but after a few hours of running I was amazed to find that I was looking attractive. To the millions of flies who call the Simpson Desert home, that is. I hadn't thought to buy a fly net and was regretting it badly, as I seemed to swallow one of the pesky little devils with every breath. The runner in front of me had his back smothered in the little buggers. By then, I was suffering from 'runner's brain' and for some obscure reason thought I could calculate how many flies must live in the Simpson Desert. I started on the basis that in our small five square metres there were, say, ten thousand flies plus those I had consumed. Now, to extrapolate that, I needed to know how big the desert was. I had no idea, so I didn't get very far in my calculations at all, but I expected that the answer would be in the zillions.

There were times out there in the middle of nowhere when I paused for a gulp of water and, looking around me under the vast skies and across the endless desert, as far as the eye could see there was absolutely nobody. How wonderful is this, I thought – total and absolute solitude.

But the brutal terrain gradually wore me down. Dune followed dune, in between which were low-lying scrub, gibber plains or even soft, shoe-sucking salt flats. The heat and the flies took their toll as well, so I was desperately glad to get into the tented village after the day's marathon effort.

The first night under canvas was a huge learning experience. It seemed that every time I needed something out of my gear bag I had to empty it all out and then repack it. In the dark, with a headlamp, this proved hopelessly impractical and very frustrating. My tent mates, however, had a lot more camping experience and their bags were properly organised with labelled plastic containers. My clothes seemed to spread out everywhere and I had to keep moving things off of the others' sleeping bags. On top of that there was the cooking and cleaning routine to get used to, sharing the limited resources with the other runners and volunteers – but by the end of the race I was much more organised in the camp.

Incidentally, the organisers of the Big Red Run event provided the tents that three of us runners had to squeeze into, as well as a roaring campfire every night and a constant supply of cold and hot water. The latter was essential for our freeze-dried food but there wasn't enough for personal washing, so we were all filthy and smelt pretty bad by the sixth-day finish. But as we were all in the same boat, it didn't seem to worry anyone.

The three of us, squeezed into Tent 14 for the race's duration, bonded together very well and, given that I am sure they both found my mess annoying, it has been a delight that I have stayed friends with both Markus and Gerry, sharing other adventures with them.

Somehow, in those cramped conditions, we all seemed to get enough sleep, but it was less pleasant when we needed to go for a pee during the night. This involved the somewhat complicated procedure of wrestling out of the sleeping bag, finding shoes which seemed to have moved, putting on warm clothes in a very restricted space, climbing over recumbent tent mates, unzipping the tent flaps, putting on the headlamp and finding your way to the distant Portaloos. Then, job done, it was just a matter of doing all that in reverse. On these perambulations, it was common to see other runners staggering about the campsite with the same mission in mind. Given these difficulties, it is understandable that some runners just went around to the back of their tents.

After the marathons on the first two days, through such rugged terrain, I was feeling so desperately low and sorry for myself. When I could manage to call home, I was crying from the total and utter exhaustion, the pain of open blisters on both feet and toenails that had lifted and parted company from me. Even my shoulders were sore where the backpack had rubbed itself over the many hours of running. The pain cave had never looked so deep and despairing.

Dale, as she always does, lifted my spirits, but each day I would stand at the start not knowing how I could shuffle one kilometre let alone forty-one more. I didn't even dare to think about the long fifth day, with eighty-four kilometres to get through. Of course, everyone involved in the BRR was very supportive and helped you where they could, but there was a limit to what I could expect from others. So each day it was a matter of applying my mind and simply putting one foot in front of the other over and over and over again. The end would come eventually. It was essential that I stayed in the moment and just let happen what would happen. Crucially there were no time cut-offs so, as long as I stayed vertical, I felt that I would get through by the skin of my teeth.

The sun beat down relentlessly for all six days with incredibly bright skies that reminded me of some of Vincent Van Gogh's oil paintings from Arles in the south of France. The desert was an interesting mix of palettes (sticking to painting terminology); apart from the red, rocky gibber plains, there were the endless dun-coloured dunes, low grey-green scrub with hardened leaves that scratched your legs and, of course, Big Red itself, which stood over forty metres high, along which we were privileged to run for a few kilometres, sinking up to our ankles in the softest of sands the colour of a magnificent sunset. A photograph which I keep even now as the screen saver on my PC shows a group of us – Rebecca, Tanya, Zac, Ian and I – so very proud to be on the top of Big Red, having gone through so much to get there. That photo continues to inspire me every time I switch on my laptop.

On the third morning, I awoke in my sleeping bag with my blow-up mattress completely deflated. There was a slow leak that I wouldn't be able to repair until I got home. My body felt as if it had slept on a park bench someplace bad. I struggled out of the sleeping bag like an overturned tortoise, feeling a tremendous sense of achievement at this very basic but critical step, and staggered out into the brilliant, chilly sunlight clutching my cup and a sachet of coffee. Before I could even think about having anything more substantial, I had to have my caffeine fix.

In the back of my mind was the knowledge that we had the third marathon ahead of us that day, but it was impossible to focus on that when my body ached all over and what used to be my two feet were in total denial mode. It was at that point that I reached for two Panadol. We had been strongly warned in the pre-race talks about the dangers of using anti-inflammatories or other pain-masking drugs, but thankfully Panadol was not considered a problem. Mind you, things were so bad it took an awful lot of self-discipline to leave the Ibuprofen in my bag.

The greatest test of all, however, came during the eighty-four kilometre fifth day. By then, most of us (maybe not the top guns) were already at our limits. I felt as if someone had put a torch to my feet and scorched the skin off. I had covered them in Fixumoll tape, but it seemed to make little difference. My numb or totally fried brain was nagging me constantly that enough was enough. It was impossible to stop the internal chatter telling me that I had done as much as I could, I didn't need to do any more and I deserved to put my feet up and have a rest.

Such mental demands to quit are tough to listen to but, as my wife will tell you, I have never been a good listener. All I knew was that I had to counter this with positive talk. Simply talk out loud to myself with total belief that I could and would do this. 'Just start and put one foot in front of the other and you'll get there in the end. You're strong and a bloody marvel. You can do it.' I knew that if I didn't put positive thoughts to the fore, I was doomed. I had never failed to finish an event I had started, and I was determined that this epic adventure across the sweltering sands and foot-destroying gibber plains would not be the first.

Talking of pain, the organisers set up a blister clinic each morning and evening. It had the look of a scene from MASH. There was always a long queue waiting for our wounds to be dressed by volunteer doctors and nurses. I remember an afternoon when one of the better runners had gone to get help, as a large part of the sole of one of his feet had lifted off in one big blister. He was obviously in great distress. The doctors told him that the only real solution was to use super glue to fix it back on. All I heard were the man's blood-curdling screams of pain. I've never heard such a terrifying sound. Amazingly, he recovered and the treatment worked well enough for him to be back out there the next day. Despite that, I had no hesitation in deciding that glueing was not going to be the answer for my feet.

So it was, on that challenging fifth day, I found myself trying to shuffle along after the gun went off. My first few steps were agony and it was clearly going to be one hell of a day. The rocks underfoot twisted my feet inside my shoes, hurting my open blisters so much that, after a short while, I was forced to power hike using walking poles (which I would highly recommend to anyone) over the feet-destroying gibber plains, down soft sandy tracks, over slippery dunes where we encountered wild camels and ostriches.

A surprised ostrich slipped over in front of us as it turned to run when it first saw a group of dishevelled-looking runners bearing down on it. The bird recovered quickly and disappeared over a dune looking a little embarrassed.

As you can imagine, I was with those runners near the back of the pack but I did eventually catch up with a lovely young lady, Pippa Lyon, who like me was struggling mightily with destroyed feet after four days of hard effort. We listened to each other's stories of pain and suffering. It was clear to both of us that we had to help each other get to the finish. Her company helped me incredibly.

After forty-odd kilometres, I was literally on my knees. I didn't think I could get back up again. It felt so good just lying inert in the shade of a lone small tree. Nothing could beat that – not even a piña colada next to a swimming pool in the Bahamas. Fortunately, Pippa remained outstandingly strong; she wouldn't let me capitulate, pulled me up and gave me a big hug of encouragement. We continued across gibber plain after gibber plain, making each step agony – but eventually, somehow, the mind processed the pain to become 'normal' and ultimately became something slightly less than unbearable.

We pushed on as the sun set over yet another huge gibber plain where the uneven rocks, magnified by shadows from our headlamps, made even hiking appear impossible. We fell into a strained silence as we both withdrew into our separate worlds, just concentrating on the next step and surviving what seemed to be an endless exercise.

The pinks of the sunset disappeared and night fell suddenly as we were searching for the next aid station, but it refused to appear. Finally, we crested a dune and there it was, with a roaring log fire and a wonderfully welcoming cup of hot tea and a slice of fruitcake. Sitting close to the fire, getting warm at last, I wanted to see what state my swollen and painful feet were in, and perhaps put more tape on them, but was too scared to take my shoes off in case I couldn't get them back on again. It was desperately hard to leave the aid station crew, who were so supportive and helpful, but Pippa and I were even more desperate to get it all over and done with. And so we pushed on, like boats against the current.

At one point, after we had left the final aid station, we climbed to the summit of a small dune and we could see the sacred lights of the finishing campsite and, it seemed, could almost touch them. It wouldn't be long now, we said happily to each other, and started to lift our pace. Well, maybe it wasn't much more than a snail could achieve.

Distances in the desert at night proved to be very deceptive and the lights we could see remained out of our reach for what seemed like an eternity. But nineteen hours after the start, under a full and huge, strangely silver moon, we crossed that distant finish line and I was a hero (to myself anyway).

Should you ever read this, Pippa, I'd like you to know that you were the sole reason that I got to the end of that horrendous day and collected my Big Red Run medal the next morning. Thank you so much. One day, I hope that I can return the enormous debt I owe you.

The final day's distance was only six kilometres and wasn't regarded by the organisers as a race. Rather, we were meant to slowly jog or even walk it, enjoy each other's company, and just get back to the Birdsville Hotel, where an Esky of cold beer had been laid on for us. Needless to say, I hobbled there in a fair bit of pain and found it hard to believe that I didn't have to go another step once I crossed that line. The finisher's medal I received seemed to weigh a ton.

When we eventually returned by bus to Adelaide, I was lying on the hotel room floor back in civilisation, with my feet up the wall eating a large tub of Nutella straight from the jar with a large spoon, and feeling my age. Resting there, I was able to fully reflect on the events of the past few days and come to terms with what, at the time, had felt like a bit of a failure. I had hiked more than I had expected and suffered far more pain than I thought I could endure.

Lying there with a mouthful of Nutella, however, it became clear to me that I had done everything I could and it was what it was – a great adventure. I had run and hiked two hundred and fifty kilometres across the Simpson Desert with some amazing people. A great achievement in anyone's book. I wanted to go back and do it again to prove to myself that I could cope with the adversity of it all a bit better, but that would have to wait for another day, as there were other places I wanted to run.

It seems very strange to me that, with a boyhood love of the green lush places in England, I should feel such an affinity for the desert country of Australia. It feels like it's in every pore, part of me. Perhaps it's the limitless horizons and the distinct lack of people. Perhaps it's the colours and the heat, but whatever it is I will always be excited to go back.

As I had become older and certainly slower in my running speed, it became clear that I was more suited to the longer events that had generous cut-off times and, in particular, I had found that multi-day races gave me what I wanted. They were in great parts of the world, well organised, and there were like-minded people to share them with. I made some lifetime friends at the Big Red Run and felt that I belonged to this fantastic tribe of special people, the ultra running community.

9

Down the Trail

'It's not what you do once in a while, it's what you do day in day out that makes the difference.' – Jenny Craig

I rediscovered the joy of trail running after I had retired to Flinders Island. As I have mentioned earlier, it was just after our loss of Allison, when the whole family was looking for solace.

It didn't take me long to remember a sandy fire trail near our home that wound through tea trees and gum trees, past white sand beaches, across knee-deep creeks and up into the hills of a national park where wallabies and wombats, as well as wild pigs, roamed. There were plenty of rocks and roots, which sometimes turned into mean-looking tiger snakes to add to the distraction. I wouldn't see a soul for hours. In the mood I was in, it was better to keep clear of people, so I avoided running on the gravel roads around our home. I wanted complete solitude for at least a short while each day.

At first, I went down the bush track on my own but as I got stronger mentally over the next few weeks, I took our dog Suzie with me, and her company helped; she brought a smile to my face now and then as her character shone through, unaware of my personal trauma. Her company did, however, pose a bit of a problem. Suzie always ran about ten steps ahead of me (just in case I got lost, I guess) and, without seeming to notice, would simply jump over any snake lying across the track. Unfortunately, by the time I got there, the snake had reared up and was ready to strike. So I had to remain extremely vigilant, especially in the summer months.

In those early days, being out in the natural world and running to my limits allowed my body to gradually regenerate and, in turn, cleared my mind of many stressors. Being aware of the relief that running gave me, I pushed myself to run further. Sometimes, it seemed that I was becoming even more introverted, but I knew that I was finding my real self and becoming whole again.

Running on the trails in the remote and wild corners of Flinders Island still does that for me. And you never know what you might encounter. One day, when I turned a corner out along a particular trail a few kilometres from home, I very nearly ran into a huge white-bellied sea eagle, holding a small wallaby in its claws, trying to take off towards me. I still tremble with the excitement I felt that humid morning, as the sea mist was lifting and the gum trees along the way dripped with moisture. I could almost touch the outspread wings of that magnificent bird as it rose above my head.

So I began to lean towards running and exploring more trails around the place. It felt right to be jumping over fallen trees, hopping over slippery boulders or wading through swollen creeks as much as shuffling along on soft sand or, even better, over the string-like leaves of the she-oak trees, which deadened the sound of my feet to such an extent that the sound of my breathing dominated my world.

Unlike running on roads, I don't feel bad about stopping for a photo opportunity or admiring the view for a minute or two. Time doesn't seem to matter out there in the wild. I may have promised my wife I'd be away for only a couple of hours, but sometimes I am led astray into the Bermuda Triangle of bush trails only to be regurgitated hours later, feeling a little sheepish, as the dog and I crawl home, dirty and tired.

I always have a feeling that any particular trail run could turn into a grand adventure. I never got that with a run on the roads, even in such a remote place as Flinders Island, where the traffic is infrequent and everyone waves as they drive past. There are no traffic lights and not a single roundabout here to get in your way, but a road is a road and it has a set destination. On the other hand, trails offer freedom.

Trail running has become a big thing in the worldwide running community in recent years. In my memory, races were traditionally on the road or even on the four-hundred-metre track, but, gradually, running in the wilderness, mountains, deserts or bush tracks has gained an increasing number of disciples. Both Chris McDougall's book *Born to Run* and *Ultra Marathon Man* by Dean Karnazes have greatly publicised the wonder of such pursuits. More and more social runners are finding how amazing trail running can be and are entering races over such distances as fifty kilometres, fifty miles or even a hundred miles (a hundred and sixty kilometres). Race directors are happy to encourage any of us to get out there and the cut-off times are, in most cases, very user-friendly. As a regular back-of-the-packer, I have never felt pressure timewise in any of the races I have entered. Sure, I have got to an aid station later in the event only to find there's nothing left to eat, or that the aid station itself has closed up and everyone has gone home, but that's never fazed me. I am still in the race, in more ways than one. And, of course, I try to ensure that I only enter those events where there are generous cut-off times, but sometimes it's difficult when that indestructible feeling comes over me.

I entered the Marysville Ultra in 2016 with my running buddy Gerry Santamaria, who I had tented with in the Simpson Desert event. This annual race is organised by Brett Saxon (who has a tremendous reputation for great events throughout Victoria) and held to support the Marysville community after the terrible events of the wildfire that swept away their township a few short years before. The regenerated Marysville is nestled among some wonderful trees and it's interesting to stroll down the tree-lined main street for a coffee and to investigate the unusual shops.

We had driven up into the foothills of the Dandenongs, where Marysville sits, the day before, enjoyed a quiet evening with a couple of cold ones and got to the start area in the morning with plenty of time to spare. It was good to catch up with some of the older faces in the crowd that I had known over the years, before we were sent on our way by the dinging of a cowbell.

I had been told that there were a few hills in this race, but I hadn't expected to be walking up a nasty incline within a few minutes of starting. Rather than entertain negative thoughts at that early stage, I reasoned that every up must have a down since the start line was also the finish. As I was towards the rear of the field (all right, the very rear), taking it easy wasn't going to be a problem; all I had to do, I told myself, was survive and get to the end in a vertical state.

This plan fell apart as the morning progressed. As the sun smote down on my thinning hair, I could feel my energy draining away, despite fuelling well and keeping hydrated. A stupid trip on the smallest of stones upset my equilibrium in more ways than one and, for a while, I seemed to stagger more than shuffle.

At the forty-kilometre aid station, I was knackered after struggling through a series of tough hills. I thought about pulling out but the volunteer, damn him, smilingly told me that it was pretty easy through the last ten kilometres to the end. He encouraged me to buckle down and keep going. Although I was a little suspicious, I took him at his word and shuffled on.

Right around the next corner was the steepest hill on the whole course. It was hands on knees, power hiking upwards for five kilometres as the sun reached its zenith and bore down through the trees. The buzz of the cicadas was deafening. The humidity seemed pretty gnarly too, and I had to stop and suck deep breaths down before pushing onwards and upwards, ever upwards. But, lo and behold, at the very summit there was the final aid station and they were handing out icy poles. I grabbed a red one and headed down towards the finish, feeling like I had turned a corner mentally as well as physically (which indeed I had). I was able to run pretty steadily from then on and even overtook one or two people before collapsing over the line just ahead of the cut-off.

Gerry had finished well before me and had enough time, I think, to shower and eat a five-course meal. It was certainly tougher than I had thought it would be and I was very conscious of not having done enough hill training in the lead up to Marysville.

Over the last few years on Flinders Island, I have been privileged to represent the community on our local council. Our small community of nine hundred souls survives on the volunteers who keep everything running smoothly. Being a councillor is one of my ways of supporting the people who live on the island. I have now been an elected member for fifteen years and enjoyed a large part of it, although there have always been difficult decisions to make and difficult people to deal with. At times, I was pushed to the limits of my patience and fortitude. My daily trail runs have definitely acted as a form of meditation and helped me get through such difficult times.

10

Running In Circles

'Start where you are. Use what you have. Do what you can.' – Arthur Ashe

In the distance, I could hear a car horn blaring. At last, it stopped. But then my car door burst open and some bloke was shaking me. I had fallen fast asleep at the wheel just as I was leaving the park. When I had got into the car, I felt OK but just waiting at the park gate for a gap in the traffic pushed me over the edge. I apologised to the concerned citizen staring in at me, turned the car around and went straight to sleep in the car park.

But I've got a bit ahead of myself; let me go back a few years to explain how that all came about. After all, I don't like to think of myself as such an irresponsible person.

That bizarre behaviour had all been brought about by circular motion. That is, running round and round a four-hundred-metre track in western Sydney. But before that embarrassing moment I had worked hard for years in preparation for such demanding track running.

It had all started back in 1983 at the Victorian fifty-kilometre championship. It was with awe that I lined up next to the perennial Cliff Young on the inside lane of the running track at Box Hill. I had watched Cliff's many heroic runs over the years and was proud to be there alongside him, hoping that some of his magic would rub off onto me. As a back-of-the-packer, I certainly had no aspirations or expectations of any great achievement but I had entered the race to see how an experienced long-distance runner would handle a track race. If my memory is correct, a very youthful Pat Farmer also ran in the event (when I think about what those two great running ambassadors achieved in their careers and, indeed, what Pat is still doing, it makes such an experience even richer).

It was a cool blustery day with intermittent sunshine. Going down the back straight of the four-hundred-metre track into the wind every lap was hard work but I found that I enjoyed the overall experience, especially when Cliff, in his inimitable fashion, croaked words of encouragement as he passed me. In that fifty-kilometre event, both Cliff and Pat showed me how patient and focused on the long term you had to be if you were to achieve your goals.

Of course, I had my usual struggle discovering what nutrition and hydration my body needed, but I was learning. And it was fantastic to see how the experts were going about everything.

While that race was a fixed distance, I had been considering for some while entering a timed event. These are usually run over eight, twelve, twenty-four or even forty-eight hours. They are in a class of their own and offer a totally different running scene that I was eager to experience. Shuffling around that Victorian track for a few hours had given me a taste of what to expect.

Most of these timed events take place on suburban tracks. Oval running tracks, that is. The surfaces can be made of different materials; some are grass or crushed gravel, while others retain the bouncy feel of synthetic Olympic-style tracks.

I have grown to love these timed events around a looped course. Apart from the ease of organising your food and drink, the main advantage, I believe, is that you are seeing other runners all the time. They are passing you or you are passing them and quite often that's when people will walk or shuffle alongside you for a chat. Sometimes, these chats last for a few minutes or other times it can be for a few hours. From arriving at the race not knowing anyone, you can leave knowing everyone's personal history. It can be eye-opening to say the least. Time seems to pass quicker too, especially through the night. During trail races, you can be out there alone for many hours and in the dark it can be quite daunting not seeing a soul, wondering if you're on the right trail and feeling psychologically beaten up. But seeing others at night in these track races is truly uplifting and in all those I have done I have never got lost!

I started my training programme one summer Sunday by running a hundred laps around a cricket oval, experimenting with some different foods. By the end of that session, I felt fairly confident that I was going to be able to handle a twelve-hour or even a twenty-four-hour race, but I'm not at all sure what the cricketers on the field made of all my effort. Even some of my running friends thought such events were ridiculous and warned me against doing them, but that me even more determined.

Back in 1991, I was still running road marathon after road marathon but I somehow became fascinated by these alternative ultra marathon track events. It was like a subculture existing under the radar of the regular running calendar and, as they were certainly less popular than marathons were, they held a real attraction to me. By the time 1991 rolled around, and I had completed a few ultra events, I was ready to tackle a twenty-four-hour track race which, I told my friends, would take me all day to finish.

I found the ideal race out at the Campbelltown Oval in western Sydney and took my place in a field of about twenty runners who looked so much more prepared than I did. But the truth was that I had done a lot of extra-long, slow distance training for nearly a year. That was at the time of my marriage breakdown when I was making my nocturnal perambulations around Sydney.

As a lead up to the twenty-four-hour run I entered the Macquarie Fields twelve-hour track race, in western Sydney. I wanted to gain experience of running through the night and greater insight into how others dealt with the situation. I was delighted to cover 92.4 kilometres in that event but was well aware that the twenty-four-hour race would be an entirely different ball game.

One of the drawbacks of such track events was that, under the rules of entry, you had to provide one or more people to sit and count your laps for the whole race. There was no such thing as electronic lap counting back then. I can't imagine how tedious such a voluntary job could be, just sitting waiting for a runner to shuffle around the course every few minutes and to write the lap time down. It would have been particularly difficult in the middle of the long night, when I recall that the temperatures tumbled. I still have the spreadsheet today with all my splits written by a very helpful workmate, Colin Townsend, who generously gave up his weekend to be there.

Throughout our years of running, we are always greatly indebted to the volunteers who give up so much to be involved in our (let's face it) very selfish sport. They fully deserve our applause and recognition for their generosity. I hope that I have thanked every one of them as I have passed by.

We started that Campbelltown twenty-four-hour race mid-morning when the temperature was already high, around twenty-five degrees, but it was to get very warm (thirty-two) and humid by mid-afternoon. I took it very conservatively, being a virgin at this and well aware that the unforgiving hours were stretched out in front of me. Shuffling lap after lap with regular walk and food breaks helped me maintain a position in the middle of the pack but naturally I remained nervous about what was to come. Being on a flat surface, I was using the same muscle groups all the time and was aware that this could cause me problems. I kept monitoring my body and tried to remain positive, reminding myself of the long, lonely night-time runs I had done leading into the race.

By the time darkness had fallen and the heat and humidity had dropped to manageable levels, I had been on my feet for ten hours and was feeling it. My hamstrings felt quite tight, so I increased my walking breaks but, eventually, I was forced to go off the track for a rest. I remembered to tell my lap counter not to expect me for a little while and climbed into the sleeping bag on the rear seat of my car, set the alarm and was in the land of nod straight away. Ten minutes later, I was fully awake before the alarm went off. I was somehow feeling a little better and, after a pleasantly invigorating cup of coffee and a biscuit or two, was ready to go again. Strange how such a short sleep can work wonders. Perhaps it was more a respite for the mind than the body but, whatever it was, I found I could run around the course strongly, feeling like I could keep it up forever.

In the middle of the night, many runners seemed to be feeling the pinch. Nobody wanted to talk very much but preferred to go within themselves as they jogged or walked around the track hour after hour. Some of them had blankets round their shoulders and looked to be in a trance as they shuffled along. It brought to mind some of those old-time marathon events in the USA that I had read about that went on until the last man or woman was standing.

One or two competitors told me they had even hallucinated, seeing weird things during the night. A phantom policeman jumped out in front of one of them and placed the runner under arrest. Sadly, I didn't have any such entertaining sights, I just fell asleep for a few seconds while running. That was weird enough.

When a fragile dawn broke over the track, I was miraculously still feeling strong. With two hours to go before the finish, my lap scorer Colin informed me that I was only a little behind the tired-looking person in fourth place. I stupidly pushed harder and harder, lap after lap, until I eventually caught him. In the end, I covered well over the hundred miles (which is about a hundred and sixty kilometres) that had been my ultimate goal, so I was naturally very proud of my achievement.

But I paid the price for overdoing it. Not only did I have that embarrassing sleep at the wheel of my car but all the obsessive training, as well as pushing so hard at the end of the race, broke me. A serious injury to my groin put paid to running for several frustrating years.

Time passed slowly but 2018 saw me happily ensconced in my second running career on Flinders Island. I had once more run a few ultra marathons by then, as well as my fund-raising runs, and was looking for a new kind of adventure. I started to think about dipping my feet back into the muddy water of such timed races.

And so I found myself at the beginning of that year scouring the cyber waves once again. Reading about the Caboolture (Queensland) 12/24/48-hour race stopped me in my tracks. I had wanted to enter that event many years before but it had somehow never fitted in with my schedule. It takes place around a five-hundred-metre crushed gravel 'road' through a very interesting historical village which has a wonderful collection of old buildings including a hospital, railway station, a blacksmith's and some old wooden council chambers.

Without hesitation I rushed off my entry to the twenty-four-hour version of the race and upped my OFR training for a few weeks. Long and slow was the order of the day, with little hill or speed work to supplement it. I deliberately included a lot more walking than usual, since I still remembered from Campbelltown how tough continuous running could get later in these events. I was fortunate that the increase in training didn't cause any additional wear and tear on my body. Pleasingly, this showed that going slower and longer was working, apart from making me more tired than usual, and giving me a good excuse for an occasional afternoon nap.

After travelling up to Brisbane, where I stayed with another old running friend, Will Cox, and his charming wife Gloria, I was poised to start the race at the crack of dawn the next morning. Will dragged himself out of bed at some ungodly hour, kindly drove me an hour up the road to Caboolture and, more by luck than judgement, we found the right place. Being the first to arrive, I was able to take my time setting up my aid station on the steps of the council chambers. I chose that spot because it looked like being in the shade for a good part of the day and it seemed a good omen, as I was a councillor myself at that time.

A couple of black coffees from the nearby café kick-started the freezing morning as I sat in the weak sunshine, waiting to defrost a bit before the start. The race director gave us the briefest of briefings and, before I could conjure up any of the usual start line worries, we were off. It was a bright and crisp start at eight a.m., with quite a few relay teams taking part but, disappointingly, only a handful of us in the twenty-four-hour solo version of the event.

As we went around the course, which sloped down slightly from north to south, we gradually got to know and support each other. From feeling a little self-conscious at the beginning, I quickly felt at ease. As hour followed hour, the morning passed easily, even though it had become quite warm and the sun was burning this old Tasmanian's pale skin. Somewhere near lunchtime, a spectator generously brought me an iced drink from the trackside café and that little can of bliss helped me through a pretty flat stage. I had shuffled and walked for more than forty kilometres and knew that I wasn't even halfway towards my hundred-kilometre goal. My thoughts kept turning to the nineteen hours ahead of me.

By then, I had met Wassa. He hadn't achieved OFR status yet and wasn't built like the usual ultra runner. However, Wassa had an extraordinary history of fund-raising for charity when, among other challenges, he endured such tortures as twenty-four hours on a treadmill. Now, that's crazy stuff. He was keen to have company that day, so we were able to help each other get through the blues over the next few hours.

This was where I got especially fortunate, as he was being looked after by his friend, Judy Angus, who had set up the best-looking aid station I have seen in all my years of running. Judy had erected trackside a huge marquee with everything you could imagine, including an electric heater for the night and a gas fire stove with two burners. Out of the kindness of her heart, Judy also took me under her wing and every lap she was there giving support to Wassa and me. At one point in the middle of the long, long night of shuffling along, she even cooked us up some wonderful pancakes smothered with Nutella. What bliss. Somehow, knowing someone was looking out for me with kind words every lap helped keep me going through the bad patches that invariably occurred.

Somewhere in the middle of that chilly night, my body forced me off the track and I went to have a brief nap in Judy's tent right next to the electric heater. I thought that half an hour would refresh me, but within a few minutes I realised that my legs wouldn't stop moving. There was no way that they were going to allow me to get any sleep, so I dragged myself back out into the darkness. It took a lap or two before I could break back into my standard old fella's shuffle, but then I felt a weird surge of energy fire up my legs. It seemed like I could run forever. I smiled and waved wildly at the lap scorer every time I passed. Where that change came from I had no idea, but I was going to milk it for all it was worth.

At the time, Kris Ryan, the only female in the race, was regularly lapping me like a machine. Kris encouraged me every time she passed and we got to know each other quite well as time wore on. She was visiting the area from Ireland (even though she's an Aussie) and had the goal of completing a hundred miles in the twenty-four hours. On the other hand, I had a much more modest aim of a hundred kilometres, with the added hope of reaching a hundred and fifty if all went well. As it turned out, Kris eventually passed her target and, pleasingly, was crowned overall winner of the event, while I was proud to be second male finisher with a distance of a hundred and forty kilometres. I don't think that I could have run any further, although if pushed I could have hiked for the last hour or two. Feeling absolutely done in, all I really wanted to do was sit, enjoy a piping hot cup of tea, courtesy of Judy, and wait for the eight a.m. finishing bell to sound.

I had finished with a smile, blister-free and an undeniable thirst for a cold beer even at eight o'clock in the morning. My friend Will picked me up, and took me back to his place, where it was wonderful to simply sit still and rest. A memorable trip it would be wonderful to repeat.

11

Beyond My Limits

'What would life be if we had no courage to attempt anything?' – Vincent Van Gogh

The young fair-haired Doctor Alex looked down at me. 'David,' he said with a wry smile on his face, 'you're nearly seventy, why can't you stop running these silly distances? What's wrong with five-kilometre races and that kind of thing? You can't keep doing this.'

I was lying in our small but modern island hospital, hooked up to some sort of machine that gave occasional beeps. The doctor had diagnosed pneumonia after I had virtually collapsed in the street and was dragged into the hospital by a worried passer-by.

The reality was that I had returned home to Flinders Island from the sixty-four-kilometre Tarawera race in New Zealand just a couple of days before. I'd been feeling a little sore in the ribs but was quite proud of the fact that my legs had recovered quickly from the mud fest that the race had been. Clearly, I hoarsely whispered to the doctor, it couldn't have been the nine hours I spent out in the bush being soaked to the skin by cold rain, blasted by severe winds or sliding on my bum in sticky, slippery mud. Mud that wouldn't let go of my shoes or let me stay vertical for very long.

'I must have caught it on the plane coming home,' I told him.

Neither he nor my long-suffering wife believed me, I'm sure.

It had taken me a week or so to fully recover from my previous race, the Big Red Run, and be back chasing my dog down the fire trails near home. The blisters that had ruined my feet were the principal culprits.

I had to wear thongs for days as I limped around the house feeling sorry for myself, much to Dale's amusement. Although I was physically recovering, my mind was struggling with the Ultra Blues, that quite serious condition where you can't find a true diagnosis until you've checked out the online ultra calendar to see what race you should register for next.

Of course, there is a plethora to choose from, so you have to decide when, where and what your budget is (this is particularly relevant to me, as it costs nearly A$400 to get to and from the island with our local air service). Plus it's hard to know what race distance will suit you so soon after pushing yourself to your limits but, hey, these are all good problems to fret over.

I had already talked to a few of my new found friends at the Big Red Run about what to run next, so I was delighted to get an email from Kim Denwer saying he was very keen to go to New Zealand to race the Tarawera Ultra early in 2016. This appealed to me as I had never raced in New Zealand, it was a mere sixty-four-kilometres and it wasn't going to be too expensive. The arrangements were made quickly and the two of us eventually flew over to Auckland for this next adventure.

The Tarawera sixty-four-kilometre ultra event that brought me to my knees was the kind of adventure that I have always loved, as it is run through some magnificent rugged country. This popular race has been held for a few years in Rotorua, a region of seismic activity – the whole town and surrounds have an atmosphere that smell of bad eggs and just walking around doesn't feel like a healthy pursuit. Fortunately, Kim and I had arrived a couple of days before the race and were able to get used to the smell, although I don't think either of us was totally convinced that the odour was solely from the local geological sources.

There was a fantastic pre-race expo held in the ballroom of a large hotel not far from the town where there were many things to look at and buy. Running is one of those sports where everyone loves to have the latest gear, gadgets and race-related memorabilia, so I had a great time indulging my passion and charging my credit card. Plus I met up with a few old running mates and enjoyed a coffee or two with them in the afternoon, which helped keep the race day nerves at bay. But as we looked out of the rain-flecked windows of the hotel, the dark grey clouds hung ominously over us, smothering the surrounding mountains we were going to run through. The news was that the region had suffered heavy rainfalls over the last few days. It was hard not to be concerned about the day ahead.

On the evening after the expo, the organisers had a fun event planned. It was a rogaine, which is a bit like a treasure hunt, where you run in pairs and follow a simple map to find hidden spots within a time limit. The more difficult locations to find attract higher points. We were waiting at the start line and a group of us were chatting to a couple of guys who had come over from Scandinavia principally for the weekend's races. Anyway, they were charming to talk to and modest in their approach to trail running in general and this event in particular. It was only much later, at the presentation after the big race, that we saw one of them on the podium. It turned out he was Jonas Buud, a Scandinavian who is one of the world's top ultra runners. In what other sport can you get to mix with the elites, and in what other sport would those same elites be so disarming and happy to talk to us back-of-the-packers as though we were their equals?

Rotorua has a wonderful food street in the heart of town and it seemed as though every runner turned up at one restaurant or another, so we had a great time getting to know each other over a couple of beers and some fine fish and chips (or 'fush 'n' chups' as they say over there). But the favourite topic of conversation that pre-race evening was the weather and the concern that the heavy rain that had fallen over the last week would cause problems. Some were worried that it would slow them down, but from my point of view, speed wasn't the issue; it was purely a question of whether or not I could finish.

Race morning eventually arrived and after quickly drinking two cups of coffee and shovelling down a bowl of instant porridge at five a.m., my room-mate Kim and I went over to race HQ and caught a ride out to the start. There were three simultaneous events that day – hundred-kilometre, eighty-kilometre and my sixty-four-kilometre race. About six hundred folk gathered under the dripping giant trees at the start line, clad in rain jackets and gloves and carrying the mandatory gear in their backpacks.

The rain had started up again but I found a mobile vehicle dispensing coffee and was very happy to get another shot into me before facing the day ahead. It was still dark, so we all had our head torches blazing away as the gun went off. Amid the usual loud cheers and clanging cowbells, the leaders sprinted away through the trees leaving us back-of-the-packers to break into a conservative shuffle a few minutes later.

After all the razzmatazz, an unsettling eerie silence fell over us. It may have been apprehension about what lay ahead or simply a sign that we were all focusing on settling into our rhythm at this early stage in proceedings. I was certainly feeling quite anxious, as the rain seemed to get heavier just then, and it was very clear that I was going to struggle.

It didn't take long before the procession of runners I was with hit the mud. Deep, thick, slippery shoe-sucking, dark mud. The runners in front of us had churned it all up and towards the back of the field it was a bit like trying to run in a cattle yard full of oozing manure. Indeed, a friend of mine slipped and disappeared over the side of the narrow trail, hit a tree badly and was forced to pull out of the race within the first twenty minutes. All the way from Melbourne, two days travelling, and it was all over in a few minutes. Ouch. But I guess that can always happen to any of us nutcases who indulge in such fantasies.

However, I struggled along walking in a cartoon-like slip-sliding fashion much more than I had expected to. But as I had realised early, time wasn't going to matter, finishing was the only goal worth considering. My feet were soaked from the word go, so I knew that blisters were a real possibility, especially where slippin' and slidin' in the mud was involved.

After an hour or two, I caught up with a couple of people I knew from other events and was able to chat (that is, curse the state of affairs), which helped take my mind off the conditions a little. Stupidly, though, I kept looking at my wristwatch. It seemed like time had also got stuck in the mud. Ten minutes felt like an hour and my mind was screaming in protest that I wasn't getting anywhere.

Suddenly, thank goodness, we found ourselves coming out of the muddy forest trail and onto a runnable trail around a pewter-grey lake. Dark clouds hung so low over the lake it seemed like they were touching the frigid water, on which quite large waves were pounding into the shore. A solo black duck bobbed up and down looking quite forlorn.

I broke into a shuffle and felt a little uplifted to be running again. After the first aid station, we headed back into the woods, onto another soggy and slippery mud trail, and it was back to power hiking again. Round a corner I came across a local guy lying by the trail, writhing in agony with severe cramps in a hamstring. I helped him stretch out a bit and gave him a few salt tablets that I hoped would do the trick. But I expected it would take him a while before he was able to work hard again.

As I was sitting in the final aid station, feeling totally and utterly exhausted and wondering where the energy to finish was going to come from, my cramping friend jogged into sight, looking pretty spry. After grabbing a drink and something to eat, he spotted me slouched despondently in a chair. He came over and returned the favour by lifting my spirits and encouraging me onwards. It's one of the best things about ultra running. Everyone in this special community looks out for each other, no matter what level of runner you are. I've never seen such help coming in a road marathon or other races, where it's everyone for him or herself.

And so, after nine hours of miserable, miserable conditions, I found myself crossing the Tarawera sixty-four-kilometre finish line, caked in mud from head to foot, more than ready for one of their locally brewed beers.

It was wonderful to get back to my motel room to clean up and rest. One of the great things about the motels in Rotorua is that every room has a thermal spa bath – great for soaking aching muscles and washing the mud out of my underwear (well, I hope it was mud).

The following day, surprisingly, I felt great for the Old Fart Runner that I had become. Just a little sore in the legs, but I was able to go for a long recovery walk in the morning, as well as another in the afternoon. I guess that the slowness of my run the previous day had helped. I had no sense of feeling even a little under the weather, let alone coming down with something as debilitating as pneumonia.

But by the time I had arrived back in the paradise that is Flinders Island, I knew that something was seriously wrong – but, of course, it wasn't caused by the Tarawera race. Oh no.

I was lying in the hospital for four days and, believe me, it was a real struggle to recover. I had huge doses of some pretty strong drugs and there was a brief moment or two when I doubted my resilience and wondered if I would ever make it back to full fitness. My lung capacity felt completely shot. I could hardly breathe and, yes, I felt like an old man; one who smoked a pack of cigarettes every day. But lying there, with oxygen being pumped into me, and nurses checking my blood pressure every little while, was enough to shock me out of the self-pitying doldrums.

It wasn't long before I swore that I would fight like mad to make a swift recovery and show those medics that age wasn't a barrier to running long distances. Sure, I accepted that I would be slower than the young brigade but I would be taking part and having fun, as well as discovering what I was still capable of achieving. Besides, what was the alternative?

The point is that, despite being over seventy, as well as having suffered such a debilitating illness, I am not going to let anything stop me. There will, of course, be setbacks. Serious setbacks sometimes, I am sure. But that is what they are, only setbacks. They are not reasons for giving up and sitting in front of the TV or playing lawn bowls. they are merely hurdles to get over and start training for the next adventure.

12

Rumble in the Jungle

'Twenty years from now you will be more disappointed by the things you didn't do than by the things you did.' – Mark Twain

After leaving the hospital, it took a few weeks before I was capable of exercising again. I was still taking strong antibiotics and felt very weak. I had also had a big scare and remained under its spell. But time did its healing work and, gradually, I was feeling strong enough to go for walks and then, later, intersperse them with brief running breaks. Although I still got breathless at times, I was desperate to put that dark period of illness behind me.

It was several weeks before my lungs and the medical profession allowed me to start proper training again and even longer before I felt able to run/walk anything resembling long distance. It became clear that the damage was going to be very long term, if not permanent. I couldn't avoid the fact that I was always now going to be at the back of any race, even if I could run any at all. But that reality had to be faced. Feeling somewhat apprehensive, I began a fresh run/walk training programme, starting very slowly of course, hoping to eventually be able to get a degree of fitness that would allow me once again to enter races that I would be able to complete, while giving me the excitement of challenging adventures.

Although the slowness of my recovery was frustrating, I doggedly stuck at it. I couldn't feel any day-to-day improvement but my running diary showed that I was indeed gradually getting stronger and fitter. Three months later, quicker than I had anticipated and with great relief,

I had made good progress and felt ready to start looking online for the next Big Thing, ideally another multi-day event.

There are, of course, many such great events around the world but only a limited number in or near Australia. I live in what is perhaps the best country in the world with uncountable advantages and the only disadvantage I have heard people say is that it's a long way from anywhere else. As you can imagine, some, including me, place this fact in the plus column.

My Big Red Run buddy, Markus Schar, had mentioned to me that he was going to enter a two-hundred-and-fifty-kilometre multi-dayer in Cambodia that was being organised by Global-Limits, a European organisation that specialises in such events around the world. When I checked out the Ancient Khmer Path online I found that it was a race through some of the country's more remote backwaters that included a lot of tiny villages, rice paddy fields, several mountain crossings and lots of ancient temple sites. It would suit me perfectly as there were would be virtually no time cut-offs. It was also a chance to get to meet some of the natives of Cambodia, as it looked like we would spend three nights camping in village halls and schools during the event. A unique opportunity indeed, especially as the last day would finish at the incredible world heritage site, the temple at Angkor Wat.

There was only one obstacle to this race and that was convincing Dale that I would be fit enough to run/walk it. By then, though, I was pretty sure that I would be able to demonstrate I had recovered adequately and that this was too good an opportunity to miss out on.

On our next visit to Sydney, I arranged to meet Markus and his lovely wife Uli for dinner one night so that we could talk to them about the race. Dale has always been supportive of my running, especially as I have become older (and more deranged and in need of help?), but it was important to know that she was happy about the whole Cambodian adventure before I raised my hopes too much and started training seriously.

Anyway, we had the best possible Malaysian dinner at a restaurant on Sydney Harbour and, after plying Dale with plenty of good white wine, she graciously agreed that it was a great chance for me. I was so excited but pretended to be a little ambivalent about entering quickly. I can assure you, however, that as soon as we got back to Flinders Island, I submitted my entry and paid the deposit. Once again, I was facing a few months of total planning obsession.

My book-lined study became race HQ; spreadsheets were pinned up, along with maps, lists of mandatory gear and shopping lists. My initial plan was to concentrate my training on being slow and steady, as I wanted to run a relaxed race without stress on my body, focusing on enjoying everything there was to see around me. After all, I didn't expect to be able to afford to go there again.

As it turned out, this was a wise decision since I feel that I truly took everything in and met another crowd of wonderful runners along the way. With my OFR training focused on long slow run/walks, I took a lot of pressure off myself, which was perfect. I hardly suffered from any injuries and landed in Phnom Penh, Cambodia's traffic-infested capital city, in November 2016 feeling ready for the challenge. Other runners from around the world arrived on the same connecting flight from Singapore and it wasn't long before we were bundled into a minibus and heading to our city hotel in absurdly heavy and chaotic traffic. On the bus, Markus and I soon found a fellow spirit in Maik Becker from Switzerland. We were to enjoy his company for the whole trip.

The first things that struck me were the heat and humidity. Was I really going to have to run in this soup-like air? The other thing was the Angkor beer. Always served ice-cold, the evening camps of the race were supplied with Eskies full of the golden fluid. Ironically, the water provided throughout the race was always warm.

After a day of acclimatisation and the usual gear check, a bus took us out to a tiny little village in the middle of nowhere. En route we stopped for lunch at a market where it seemed everyone was buying roasted cockroaches or barbecued spiders for a treat. During the bloody rule of the Khmer Rouge in the 1970s, the starving population were forced to eat whatever they could find. It seemed that everyone still either needed to eat such delights or they just enjoyed them. Thank god I had my regular freeze-dried food. Much as I disliked eating it, it was at least more digestible than bugs.

Our first night was a wonderful experience, one that will stay with me for a long time. We were still getting to know each other and we were thrown together in a big way when we arrived at our overnight accommodation. It was in a remote village hall, a rough wooden structure on a raised platform. Inside, a variety of coloured mosquito nets had been hung from ropes stretched across the large open space. Each runner had an area in which to sleep and keep their gear. Using the hot water provided, we all prepared our pre-race dinner and sat around eating and chatting as the darkness rapidly enveloped us.

In the middle of the night, as usual for this Old Fart anyway, I needed a pee and darted out into the nearby bush. On returning in the pitch black that is an Asian night, I mistook my neighbour's netted sleeping area for my own. I sure gave the young lady lying there a bit of a shock when I put my hand out only to find her leg where I thought my sleeping bag was. I whispered my apologies but her frightened gasp made me cringe. How embarrassing.

When the hazy dawn crept over our boudoir, the girl in question soon forgot about my poor sense of direction and was more than dismayed to find her running shoes had been stolen. Then others, much to their horror, found the same thing. Without them, their race was over before it even began. The event organiser quickly explained that the villagers were extremely poor and, although the company had made a sizeable donation to the village as a whole for the use of their hall, some of the youngsters saw us as easy game to acquire a flashy pair of joggers. After lengthy negotiations with the village chief, a small payment was made for the return of the shoes, everyone was satisfied and nothing more was said. But, needless to say, nobody let their shoes out of their sight for the remainder of the event.

After a breakfast of an energy bar, a banana and a couple of good cups of coffee (is there such a thing as a bad cup?), we sauntered over to the start, where we were sent on our way after a blessing from a group of Buddhist monks in saffron-coloured robes. Most of the next few days were spent running on bright orange gravel roads, through many shanty villages all of which sported a large red Esky outside their earthen-floored local shop. We had been told that if we were lucky we might find a cold Coca-Cola in those Eskies, but no way – firstly, there was no ice and secondly, they had every other beverage known to mankind but not a Coke to be seen. Indeed, by the time my slow colleagues and I got into each village, the store owner would come running out shouting in broken English, 'No Coke, no Coke,' because he'd been asked for it by each of the thirty or forty runners in front of us.

The course was marked each day with bright pink tape, essential when we went off-road through wooded areas or along the retaining banks of a paddy field. This system worked pretty well, until the third day, when we suddenly spotted some village kids running around with pink ribbons in their hair. Thank goodness we were able to follow some faint footprints to where the next ribbon was tied out of reach, high in a tree.

There was one particular day when we had to climb a very steep hill in tough conditions. It was too hot and humid to push hard, so I shuffled along by myself or with others but I ran out of water about an hour before I was due to get to the next aid station (a four-wheel drive vehicle at the side of the road). That hour was a real struggle. Eventually, I was forced to a slow walk feeling almost nauseous from the lack of water. When I eventually made it to the vehicle, I gulped down a whole bottle of tepid water and was told that drinks would next be available in five kilometres. I only took what I needed for such a short distance, as it would otherwise become undrinkable under the scorching sun. Unfortunately, it was a hell of a lot more than five kilometres before I could get a refill, so that by the end of the day I was desperately dehydrated, feeling very light-headed and wobbling all over the place as I walked it in. Thank goodness our campsite was by a cool, fast-running river in which I lay down fully clothed and drank the best cold beer I think I have ever had. The lesson I took away from that day was to never believe what a volunteer tells you about distance and always carry more water than you think you will need.

But generally the days' runs were extremely enjoyable, passing through rustic villages and past vast rice paddy fields where the local kids dashed out to meet us, wanting to say 'hello, goodbye' every few minutes as well as giving us high fives. The heat and humidity took their toll but we were mostly well tended along the route by the organisers and more than happy to reach the overnight finishes, where cold beer always awaited us.

At one point, I was invited into a paddy field to help the villagers scythe their rice crop. We had a lot of laughs in the few minutes I was 'helping' but it was typical of the reaction us runners got from the warm-hearted Cambodian people. It was a very special time.

The Jungle Day left a very different impression on me, however. It was a sixty-five-kilometre day. After a very early start and a bit of a hill climb, we were soon deep in among pretty gnarly trees, some of which sported large thorns about head height. The insects swarmed around our heads and I was pleased to have brought a fly net. We shuffled along a single track that I found difficult to run on, so when I met up with Melanie and Alison (we made up the M-A-D team) power hiking along, I happily stayed with them. We had a very enjoyable thirty kilometres, fording murky swollen creeks and even helping a farmer to push a bogged three-wheel tractor out of a deep slimy mud hole.

It was around lunchtime when we exited the jungle at a small village store and, lo and behold, they had a few cold Coca-Colas left in their electric fridge. Yes, they had a generator. By now it was midday and the three of us collapsed in the shade of a large spreading tree and guzzled down two Cokes each. I quickly felt rejuvenated and ready to get going again, but my two companions were feeling the effect of the heat and decided to rest and enjoy a proper meal that the store offered.

I waved the girls goodbye and pushed myself for the next few hours along the torturously straight gravel road under the scorching sun. I put in regular walking breaks for short periods to help me cope with the conditions. It felt extraordinarily good to be running again and I went very well until darkness fell suddenly, as it does in Cambodia. As often happens when night comes, I fell into a bit of a hole. I didn't have a clue as to how far I had to go, or even where the next drink station was.

Again I was fortunate to meet up with another group of runners who were as exhausted as I was and were just focusing on getting to home base. We helped each other by talking non-stop to take our minds off the endless gravel road that shone in our head torches in front of us, and eventually found our camp set up in the ruins of an eleventh-century temple. We were able to sit outside our tent in the cool evening air, eat our meals and catch up with everyone else's adventures.

Our final day was a short run (sixteen kilometres) along quiet country roads adorned with signs warning of wild elephants and pigs, which led us to the historic temple complex of Angkor Wat. Before reaching there, however, we had to pass through a couple of other wonderfully carved temples. The rule was that, to show respect, we had to just walk through them – which was great, as there was so much to see.

It was somewhat of an anticlimax to cross the finish line at the magnificent world heritage Angkor Wat and realise that it was sadly all over. Everyone was lying around in the heat, drinking from coconuts and sharing memories of a wonderful experience in a very special place. To me, it's a great shame that I can't afford to keep doing races in such exotic places, but it is what it is and I'll rest happy in the knowledge that I have at least been able to have a couple of such marvellous adventures.

The awards dinner that night in a fancy hotel was a fitting end to our time in Cambodia. It was sad to say farewell to so many of these people who had come together from all over the globe for a few days, but the next morning I was heading back to Phnom Penh ready for the flight home. I was very tired, ready for a good rest, but over the moon with what I had experienced.

Once again, I was faced with the emptiness that comes after such an exciting time when you are at home surrounded by life's normality, but still retain the excitement and adrenalin you experienced on such an adventure. But I knew that it was only a matter of time before I could have my much-needed fix.

Before I could even think about that, there was another adventure waiting for my wife and me nearer home.

13

The Edge of the World

'Running is about finding your inner peace, and so is a life well lived.' – Dean Karnazes

Somewhere in the middle of the wild seas of the Bass Strait, between our home on Flinders Island and Wilsons Promontory in Victoria, lies the tiny but exquisite Deal Island, which forms part of the Kent Group. You may find it if you scour your atlas carefully, although it's not included on every map as it's so small.

For three months in 2017, Dale and I were privileged to be sole caretakers there. We really were on the edge of the world, being isolated for most of that time. Visiting yachts were few and far between. The island is a national park (measuring only four by six kilometres) with a decommissioned lighthouse at the top of the steepest hill.

One of my duties was to keep all the bush tracks slashed and trimmed for any visitors who fancied a beautiful bushwalk. So it was only natural that I should run the tracks and wonderful that I never saw another person out there. How many people can run for at least an hour every day for three months without seeing a soul? And solitude is a wonderful thing; with connections to the outside world being extremely limited, we felt the cares of daily home life drop from our shoulders.

Most mornings, I ran up and down the quite severe hills on the little island for at least an hour, but after a few weeks I thought that it would be grand to do something a bit different that would make our stay even more memorable. And so the idea of the No Big Deal

Marathon was born, in which I would be the sole participant. The only regulation I had was that you had to be an island resident to enter, which made damned sure nobody else was going to qualify and knock me off the podium.

I spoke to the volunteer aid station manager (my wife Dale) and, after a little persuasion, the run was organised for a morning late in our residency. It was to take place on a loop I had measured to be a little more than seven kilometres. It involved opening and closing a few wallaby exclusion gates along the way, and the start/finish line would be a blue line drawn outside our little homestead, where the drinks and food table would also be set up. To be honest, it was the flattest loop I could find and it avoided any really technical surfaces but included a short beach run on each lap. I didn't want to make it difficult, I just wanted to be able to say I ran at least a marathon on such a small and remote place as Deal Island.

I had to delay the big event for a few days because of inclement weather. It pelted with icy rain, and strong winds blasted our windows, forcing me to remain indoors, frustrated not to start this particular adventure, but there was no way I was going to fight such abysmal conditions. After three days, the clouds finally cleared and allowed the sun its rightful place in the firmament.

Being the only entrant, the pressure and tension on the painted blue start line outside our temporary home were not too noticeable. Dale sounded the off just after eight a.m. and I headed out on the first of six loops feeling very relaxed. In reality, it was just another training run, albeit for 42.2 kilometres.

The course started as a jog down a steep narrow track to Little Squally Cove, where the large white-crested waves were crashing against the lichen-encrusted granite cliffs. From there, it was a fairly brisk climb back up to one of the major trails that led me onwards and downwards to the beautiful little Garden Cove at the northern end of the island. There, I ran backward and forwards along the beach before heading back to complete the circuit. As I have said, the overall loop measured about seven kilometres, and both the total ascent and descent on each was only three hundred feet, but with six laps this added up.

The only difficulty I encountered was that every time I ran up the short emergency airplane runway, which was on the way to Garden Cove, a pair of Cape Barren geese (who thought they owned the place – and probably had more right to be there than me) would aggressively charge at me with their wings outstretched, heads down and making a hell of a honking noise. I had to stop abruptly, wave my arms about and shout at them before they would back off and let me pass. Funny when you think about it – in making my gestures, I was copying exactly what they were doing. Anyway, if that was the only issue I had, there was no need to complain and, of course, there was nobody to hear me if I had.

Apart from the geese problem, the first three or even four loops went smoothly in about forty-five to forty-seven minutes each, with some water and an energy bar each time I passed the house, but after that the sun started to beat down. The climb out of Garden Cove also began to take its toll, so from then on I was forced to throw in a couple of walks on each lap. After four hours and thirty-eight minutes, I was delighted to cross the finish line feeling pretty pleased with myself.

It's not often (that is, never) that I get to stand at the top of a podium but I took the crown as modestly as I could and headed indoors for a cold, cold reviving beer and a good meal.

We shortly thereafter returned to our normal life on Flinders Island, where my thoughts inevitably turned to future efforts in the coming year, 2018.

But the best-laid plans of mice, men and runners…

14

Reality Bites

'We rejoice in our sufferings, knowing that suffering produces endurance, endurance produces character and character produces hope. And hope does not disappoint us.' – Romans 5:3–5

I was lying on a treatment table with electrodes stuck to my chest and I was panting desperately for air. Things weren't looking good. Where had I gone wrong? I had, of course, been lucky to recuperate so well from my pneumonia episode, but I thought I was past all that and could get on with my plans.

At the start of 2018, I was continuing to chase goals wherever they could be found. At times, they looked beyond me but I found it hard to see any limitations to my dreams. By and large, I managed to get through everything that was thrown at me in races, but as the ageing process was taking its toll, I grudgingly accepted that my goals needed to be more realistic.

This was brought home to me strongly in February 2018 just across the wild Bass Strait in the little village of Derby, which lies in the north-eastern corner of Tasmania. The event was called the Tassie Trail Fest and I was excited to be going for their weekend of Multi Madness.

Derby is just over a two-hour drive from Launceston and I went through some beautiful country to get there, along twisty roads passing green fields overflowing with contented cattle. The journey was marred a little by the constant rain sloshing against the windscreen of my hire car, but arriving in Derby made up for the weather. Lying in a pretty and lush green valley, it's a quaint old tin mining town that has recently been reborn as a mountain bike trail mecca. Gnarly dirt trails abound, with such haunting names as Black Dragon, Howler, Axehead and Rusty Crusty.

After a quick stop for a light lunch at a small café crowded with mud-spattered bikers, I found my way to the Derby town hall for race registration. The words 'town hall' conjure up a picture of grandeur and authority – but here in little Derby it's a single-storey wooden-clad building painted proudly in cream. Sheltered inside away from the pouring rain were two young ladies who quickly found my name on the list of registered runners and allocated me number '3'. I must have unexpectedly become an elite runner.

There were also a couple of sponsors' stands where I picked up a T-shirt as well as a good supply of gels from Hanny Allston's stand. Hanny is a well-known champion trail runner in Australia, so it was wonderful to have a brief chat with her. Hanny's huge retail stores in central Hobart and Launceston, covering every adventure sport you can think of, and her podcast, both operate under the name Find Your Feet. I am an avid listener to her widely diverse podcasts so it was great to put a face to the voice.

Geologically Derby looked an interesting place, having had large tin mines operating in the area. I would have loved to explore some of the remote corners but the slanting rain across the surrounding hillsides forced me back to my modest bed and breakfast for a rest before the first of the five events I had optimistically entered. Looking back, this was crazily beyond my abilities but all I can say is it seemed like a good idea at the time.

The opening $100 Dash For Cash was a complete disaster as far as I was concerned. Clearly, I wasn't in the hunt for any cash prize but what I got was an almost physical punch in the solar plexus. The Dash, which was over a mere one kilometre, was on a very undulating and rugged bush track that was, of course, designed for mountain bikes. It took me an outrageous twelve minutes to stagger over the finish line and I had been gasping for breath on some of the steeper climbs. I even had to walk one of them. This shook me up badly, as I had always thought of hills as my friends and I couldn't understand what had happened to me. Little did I realise that this was just a taste of what was to follow on the long second day.

Overnight, the weather remained ugly and I woke up regularly to the sound of rattling windows and the swoosh of windswept rain on the tin roof. But by the time we were at the trailhead for the start of the long race, it had faded to a mere drizzle and shortly thereafter the sun even broke through in patches. At the same time, the humidity climbed to an uncomfortable level, as the course was sheltered from any sort of breeze by the thick bush cover. I was carrying plenty of water in my running pack but over the hours of the race, it was difficult to drink enough fluid.

The trails themselves were simply the best I have ever seen. Truly. We were surrounded by gigantic eucalypt trees, some of which twelve people with extended arms would have had difficulty embracing. Many were covered in the brightest green moss, as were the many huge granite boulders, the size of houses that we dodged past. It was the middle of an ancient forest, with many of the huge trees having fallen or been felled epochs ago. These too were moss-covered. And some had large midsections removed to allow the trail through.

This race was called the Marathon and we were told it covered forty-four kilometres. In the end, however, it was measured by my running partner's GPS watch as 48.45 kilometres and 1,315 metres of 'vert' rather than the ridiculous four hundred metres detailed in the pre-race material. Add the humidity and the severity of the zigzag uphills (typical trail bike country) and things turned sour for me about halfway through. Luckily, I had caught up with a lovely young lady from Brisbane, Jemma, who was looking to take this event easy to ensure that, like me, she could finish the Multi Madness. Great, I thought, let's work together and get to the end in good shape.

For several hours, we shuffled along, happily chatting and sharing our life stories. We noticed, however, that after almost twenty kilometres we were working harder, but still conscious of the most wonderful scenery around us. Huge man ferns towered over our heads, and interlaced above them were more of the magnificent gum trees, some of which were lemon-scented, adding to the overload of our senses. We even had to run through a hole cut in a long-abandoned dam wall.

At last, we staggered out of the forest onto a large rock platform where an aid station was just about to shut down. We had been expecting this station at thirty-one kilometres and thought that it would be around every corner we came across, but it turned out to be thirty-four kilometres before we got there and could refill our water bottles. It took a lot of willpower to get going again after that. Both Jemma and I felt completely worn down by the terrain and the climate. The non-appearing aid stations didn't help, although there was nothing to do but suck it up and follow the tried and true principle of relentless forward progress.

Mostly, we kept each other motivated and positive but, inevitably, the toughness of the day brought silence down on us at times as we gritted our teeth and pushed resolutely on. It became difficult to even appreciate the beauty of our surroundings.

Eventually, the finish area appeared through the trees like a mirage and we scampered with a final spurt of energy across the line, hand in hand, equal last or, as I prefer to think of it, equal second last, in just over eight hours. So slow – ouch.

Feeling exhausted, it wasn't a difficult decision to not run any of the final events in the Multi Madness, which included a sixteen-kilometre trail run the same afternoon followed by a very hilly half marathon the next morning. Another hilly sixteen-kilometre race rounded out the weekend. My withdrawal fuelled a spiralling sense of failure surging through me. I was getting so much slower, hurting more as well as taking longer to recover. Could I keep coming back for more, I wondered.

Self-examination is a good thing at the right time, but I realised that I needed to wait a while before looking too closely at my crappy performance in Derby. So it was that, within a few days, I was back out in the wilds of Flinders Island pushing myself up hill and down dale in an attempt to be ready for my return to the Big Red Run in June 2018 that I had committed to running.

Strangely, however, I continued to feel sluggish. I was still short of breath on my hill workouts and sometimes it felt as if my heart would jump right out of my chest, just like in the Dash For Cash a short while before. I tried resting in case it was simply a matter of overtraining but that didn't help at all.

Desperately, I spoke to my local GP, Lynne Davies, who is also a keen runner – so she would have some idea about what I was facing. Perhaps, she suggested after an examination, some Ventolin might open up my airways and help my ageing body cope a little better, especially with the hill work so essential for trail running. She told me a story about many of the Olympic and Commonwealth Games runners who are medically permitted to take Ventolin with excellent results. If it was OK for them to adopt such a strategy, I shouldn't feel bad about doing the same.

Optimistically, I sucked down a couple of Ventolin lungfuls before each training run and, to a mind ready to grasp at straws, it seemed to help. What a relief. Flushed with success, I returned to the doctor to organise the certificate of good health that was required for the six-day two-hundred-and fity-kilometre Big Red Run, which was fast approaching. Here I hit an immovable obstruction as Doctor Lynne insisted that I had to take a stress test before clearing me for BRR entry.

In extremely good humour, but perhaps a little cynical about the medical profession's negativity, I flew off to Launceston and attended the recommended specialist. My torso was covered with sticky electrodes connected to a 'machine that goes ping' (as they called it in *Monty Python's Flying Circus*) and I was asked to climb onto a familiar-looking treadmill, facing a bank of computer screens. The treadmill started up slowly and I smilingly thought, 'Ah ha, I can even put this down as a training run in my logbook.' However, I was rapidly brought down to earth by the total failure of my body to cope, as the treadmill got very fast and steep towards the end of the test.

At first, I thought that I was going to be told that Ventolin was still the best recourse for me and that they would recommend that I should be given my desperately needed certificate for the BRR. I was so very wrong. As I lay on the treatment table gasping for air, it was explained that it looked as though I had Athlete's Heart. It seemed something I should be proud of but the cardiologist, Doctor Geoff Evans, made it crystal clear that it was a serious condition and I had to stop doing extreme events, including the multi-day stuff that I loved to do. He further went on to explain that I could not run for more than one or two hours at a time and, certainly, there was to be no more pushing myself hard up hills.

Apparently, my heart muscle had become enlarged over the forty years of training and running ultras and was effectively only pumping about forty per cent of the heart's volume instead of the usual minimum of fifty per cent. Bluntly I was told that if I continued to run ultra marathons there was every likelihood that I would drop dead in the not too distant future. Indeed, Doctor Evans made his case even stronger by telling me, 'You don't see many ultra runners your age…they're usually dead by now.' A sobering thought.

An additional test to get a second opinion only confirmed that my arteries were fine, but it was the overdeveloped heart muscle that was the problem. How weird is that – you'd have thought all that running would certainly have made my heart stronger, but to make it too strong? Crazy.

I felt destroyed. In one brief moment, my world had turned upside down and the thing that was central to my being was taken away. I was reduced to tears and sat there totally stunned, unable to move. I had no idea how I was going to go forward from there. Initially, I held out a faint hope that I could recover after a decent rest and start training again, but both the specialist and my trusty local doctor quickly put those hopes to bed.

I was facing the fact that the end had come. Of course, I knew it would happen some time and quite honestly recognised that at seventy-one it was going to be sooner rather than later – but not to have the door slammed in my face like this. The sword of Damocles hung over me; it seemed that I was doomed to spend the rest of my days taking life easy.

So there I was in an extremely dark place, somewhere that I hadn't believed existed. A cave that seemed to offer me no way of escape. Deep down, however, I could not accept that this was the end of my road. There was no way I could allow myself to be called an Old Fart Hiker. Totally unthinkable.

I remained in a state of shock for a week or so but, as the reality of the situation came home to me, I worked hard to mentally accept my limitations. I made an effort to be content with a brisk walk (or power hike as I preferred to call it) for an hour each day, with the excitement of a gentle run/walk every Sunday. At this point, I had cancelled my entry to the Big Red Run, which was in three weeks, as well as withdrawn from the daunting three-hundred-and-twenty-kilometre Alps2Ocean in New Zealand the following February.

In the back of my mind, I still fostered a hope that I could enter the shorter course version of the multi-day event at Larapinta in August 2018 as a run/walker. I had to have something to hang on to, something to aim for in the short term. If I could get agreement to that from Doctor Lynne, I would at least have an event to focus on and obsess about, as well as a long-term hope for the future. I knew, of course, that there was not going to be any short cut; no miracle cure – I just had to take one patient step at a time, like in any running event, towards the ultimate goal of being a runner again.

Over the next few months, I endured more tests, scans and long discussions with heart specialists. I was put on dreaded drugs that helped in a limited way. I worked hard at getting my blood pressure down, as I could see that there was a clear correlation between that and my heart rate. At the same time, I refused to lie down and become what I feared most – a couch potato. Every day, I took the dog down our favourite bush track, hiking as fast as I felt comfortable, and sometimes I even ran for short periods until my HR went above the doctor's recommended level of a hundred and forty beats per minute.

There were many days I returned from those outings sick at heart at what seemed like the total futility of it all. I even wanted to know if there were better drugs out there that would allow me to run more. For many years, I had been proud of the fact that I hadn't needed any medication, but here I was ready to consume a veritable smorgasbord of pills of every shape and colour if it meant that I could run.

After long and harrowing reflection of the emptiness left within me during this spell of non-running, I asked the Big Red Run organisers if I could be a volunteer, instead of a runner, at the 2018 event. It would mean that I could go back to the stark and wild beauty of the Simpson Desert and enjoy it all without the suffering of running for six days. Not exactly what I had hoped for but, as they say, beggars can't be choosers.

And so I returned to the tiny windswept hamlet of Birdsville in the middle of nowhere. And, yes, it was good to give back to the running community that had given me so much over the years but, at the same time, I found it very hard. Every morning, as the runners lined up to head out into the wilderness and challenge themselves through such awe-inspiring but tough terrain, I was disappointed that I was not alongside them. On the other hand, when they returned to camp, hobbling with blisters and very distressed, I was relieved that it wasn't me.

Even so, as a non-combatant, I made some great new friends and shared my tent with a truly fine bloke, Greg Hall, an ultra runner who hails from Newcastle. I had chatted with Greg on Facebook before the race and we had arranged to meet at the hotel bar in Adelaide the night before catching the bus up to Birdsville. He had sent me a photo so that I could recognise him easily. A fat lot of good that was; he looked completely different when we eventually caught up – he wasn't even wearing a cap as in the photo.

Greg was assigned to run part of the course every morning before it was raced, to ensure that all the flags and signs were in place. It required a herculean effort from him, while my role was simply standing at an aid station out in the desert, helping runners as they came past.

I did manage to squeeze in a couple of short runs out into the red sands surrounding the camp, which helped my sanity a little, but only served to further whet my appetite to get back to some adventures.

I went home from the BRR more anxious than ever to discover what my future running capabilities would be. I had long chats with Doctor Lynne. She was extremely supportive of my efforts but warned me strongly about trying to do too much, which she seemed to think all runners would do. Where she got that idea from, I'll never know.

In the end, after much perseverance, I was given clearance to run the Larapinta Trail race in August 2018. This was quite a relief as, unbeknown to anyone, I had already paid the substantial entry fee. When I say permission to run, I do, of course, mean that I would be interspersing power hiking with some running breaks when my HR permitted. Even so, I was pretty excited. Excited to be in a multi-day event again; excited to be going back to the Red Centre of Australia with Dale; excited to share the event with a large part of our family who were also going, but mostly really, really ecstatic to again be able to think of myself as someone capable of finishing an arduous outing through some of Australia's beautiful but rugged desert country.

The race website showed that the event I had entered into was over four days, with distances of only thirteen, twenty, twenty-two and thirty-one kilometres. I didn't imagine that I would be troubled too much and that I would hardly break into a sweat. Well, that was the plan but, as Mike Tyson famously said, 'Everyone has a plan – until they are punched in the mouth.' And I certainly got a huge right hook to my face on the second day.

The first evening's run was through some gentle hills at sunset using a friendly single track, finishing with a long avenue of flashing coloured lights leading up to the historic Telegraph Station, just outside the remote Northern Territory township of Alice Springs. This was a very relaxed start to the four-day event and it was pleasant to get back to the hotel and enjoy a good meal before heading to bed. As we left the restaurant, we were told that the twenty kilometres tomorrow was going to be a tough day. And they weren't kidding.

A cold start with sharply clear skies saw me shuffling along at the back of the field. I was able to run/walk the first hour or so but after that, as the terrain got worse and the heat increased, it was almost all power hiking. I was pleased to have taken my hiking poles. There were many ravines with steps built for people twice my height, followed by some awesome canyons with sculpted red rocks that reflected the midday heat down onto my sweltering body.

At one point, with only a few kilometres to go, I threw myself down under a shade tree (one of the few around) to take a break. Suddenly, out of the blue, two angels appeared in the form of race volunteers carrying large bottles of cool water and electrolytes. After guzzling a fair amount, I felt able to continue, climbing up to and over a steep ridge with a rugged downhill that required the use of poles for balance.

At long last, I reached a lovely flat sandy trail that led to the finish line and an ice-cold Coca-Cola, followed by a desperately needed cup of coffee from the nearby café at Standley Chasm. It had taken me six hours to get it done and I was exhausted. I could not believe it was only twenty kilometres – surely there was some mistake; but no, I had to face up to reality. I was slow, very slow indeed, but on the plus side I was not last, I was still in the game and smiling to boot.

Day three was a very different story, as my mate Gerry Santamaria, who had talked me into entering this event in the first place, had withdrawn from the previous day's long run with a pulled muscle somewhere in his glutes (which I wasn't going to check out). Instead, he elected to walk the short course event with me. We power hiked the whole thing and had a good day swapping stories and helping each other get the twenty-two kilometres done.

We crossed several ancient dried river beds where the rocks had been rounded by annual floodwater over the millennia. The red gorges and rocky slopes we encountered were fantastic, and it was very special to finish in the magnificent Ormiston Gorge. Afterwards, I felt amazingly fresh as we relaxed at Glen Helen Resort, deep in the red dirt of central Australia. It was a real privilege to be there taking part.

The final morning was bloody cold to say the least. After managing to get a very early breakfast and the indispensable cups of coffee, the race bus took us to the start line near the Finke River (the oldest river in the world, as my geologist wife impressed on me). Unfortunately, the bus had to return to the resort to pick up the next batch of runners and left the first load standing around for almost an hour. My fingers ached with the cold and I cursed forgetting to take my gloves.

Eventually, we got going and I was delighted to discover that my heart rate allowed me to run more. Perhaps it was taking it easy the day before that helped. In any event, I was able to keep up with a group of runners and enjoyed listening to the chat and the support that went with it. The five of us looked after each other and we crossed the line in five and a half hours. The finish was again right on the Finke River and a cold, refreshing dip in what water there was, followed by an even chillier beer, made the whole experience unforgettable.

The original diagnosis of my heart issues had occurred in May 2018 but by September that year, after completing the Larapinta adventure, I felt like there was some light at the end of the tunnel. I had discovered that I could run/walk decent distances and still be a small part of the running scene. I had, of course, accepted that ultra marathons and the tougher multi-day events were beyond me. But there were definitely days when I could run for longer periods within my heart rate limitations, and that gave me hope.

On the back of this renewed confidence in myself, I entered the Launceston Marathon in September 2018, as it was on a very flat out and back (four times) course with no time restrictions. If it became too hard, I told myself that I could always pull out at the end of a lap. I set out conservatively at the back of the field to power hike it, interspersed with regular jogs and found the whole event very enjoyable. I met quite a few old running buddies along the way and got through the whole marathon without being DFL. And the next day I was even able to go for a proper run. Boy, was I feeling a lot more positive about life and the meaning of the universe.

After that success, I was keen to find new adventures, so I arranged with Gerry and his wife Lynne to run/walk the Great Southern Rail Trail in Gippsland. It was planned as a casual and social outing over a weekend. It turned out to be a fantastic way of covering longer distances in a stress-free environment. There are a lot of similar trails throughout Victoria but this particular one is about seventy kilometres long, passing some fine, grassed paddocks crammed with dairy cattle, as well as cutting through a lot of shaded woods where the old train line had been. One of the attractions was that, being a disused rail track, the gradients were very user-friendly. There were all sorts of side attractions like vineyards, lime kilns and natural beauty spots but we just kept moving along, apart from when we passed through townships and the smell of coffee forced us to a halt.

We covered the trail in an easy two days, stopping overnight at the art deco style Fish Creek Hotel that stood conveniently at the halfway point. Gerry and Lynne were so full of enthusiasm for this region of Victoria and kept talking about other trails we could go on.

It was clear that many other adventures were waiting for me. I definitely had things to look forward to and train for.

15

A Runner's Musings

'I'm older now, but I'm still running against the wind.' – Bob Seger and the Silver Bullet Band

Now that I am a fully-fledged Old Fart Runner, I can look back on how I have approached my running over the years and see the common threads woven through it all. I have always used races as a measure of how I'm doing, and I've run the best I can in those events, but the principal purpose has been sheer indulgence – to enjoy the outing and see what I am capable of. I mean, at the ripe old age of seventy-two or -three, what else is there and, in reality, what was there in my past that was any different? I have never been in danger of getting on any genuine podium. So it has always been just a matter of experiencing the challenge, doing the best I can, as well as enjoying the company and support of like-minded runners.

Take, for example, the 2015 Big Red Run race. My two tent mates were nice guys and, although they were clearly a different class of runner from me, they were so supportive. After I finished the long day's run of eighty-four kilometres at about two a.m., Markus and Gerry had been home for hours and were exhausted from their own efforts but they still came out to cheer me as I all but crawled into camp. They had my sleeping bag and inflated mattress ready for me. I hadn't known either of these guys before but they have since become like family to me.

Throughout my running years, I have had trouble accepting the impact that external things can have on me, especially bad things. In the past, I have found it hard to stop running or, heaven forbid, miss an event if I've been injured or had to give priority to family or business matters. But now I have grudgingly accepted that I won't be able to run whenever I want to, I won't always be at maximum fitness and that I will require more rest than I did when I was younger.

Acceptance of reality has also been an issue during an ultra. I am still learning to face up to the fact that I will get in a bad and dark place at different times in a race. I do, however, recognise that this is a critical part of my running and, indeed, life in general. When I was forced through injury to stop running altogether for some years, I was very frustrated at first and enjoyed many a pity party. Like a dog with a bone, I used to sit on the balcony at home, which overlooked a path alongside the Sydney Harbour, and mope jealously as runners of all shapes and sizes shuffled or raced below me. I drove my new wife mad and eventually she had to speak strongly to me before I could see what I was doing. When I thought about it, I realised that I was wasting energy on something negative rather than sucking it up, enjoying the now and looking optimistically to the future.

So it was in 1993 that I was forced to face the fact that I couldn't run and find an alternative physical exercise that could satisfy me. The truth is that I never did find a replacement for running, especially something as beautiful as running all day in a trail ultra marathon. I tried cycling, I tried gym work, I tried simply walking, but nothing gave me the buzz that running had always provided. I had thrown myself into each of them at different times. They all worked their magic for a while, but in the long term were never going to replace my calling as a long-distance runner.

As I have mentioned earlier, it was only after I retired to Flinders Island that I was able to get back to running and feel that buzz again. At first, I couldn't believe that I could do it, but I quickly found that the initial aches and pains faded away and I could even manage to tighten my trouser belt a couple of notches. I felt much more positive in myself and better able to deal with life's many problems. Plus I started to sleep a lot better at night – with the occasional therapeutic afternoon nap thrown in.

When I look at what others have suffered, I realise that my short-term problems have been relatively insignificant. I know that many other runners have faced worse setbacks and overcome them. For example, when I hear of what the elite ultra runner Dave Mackey went through when he had a leg amputated as a result of a freak mountain running accident, and I recall what a major issue a few blisters were to me in a particular race, it's all brought into perspective. So I find it very important to accept what I am given on any day and any run and just enjoy the moment. This can, of course, be difficult at times but I try to remind myself that the joy of it all is the reason that I head out the door for a run most mornings. By the way, Dave Mackey returned to run ultras using a prosthetic.

It was at the Tarawera race in Rotorua that I bumped into a friend from the Big Red Run days, young Kirsten Maplestone. I caught up with her somewhere around the middle of the race when I recognised her usual bright, multicoloured gear and enjoyed chatting for a while. Unfortunately, she was suffering badly and we got separated. Kirsten is a legend in the Victorian ultra scene, widely known for her fortitude as well as her ceaseless support of other runners. But it's her struggles that have given me much food for thought.

When I consider what Kirsten has conquered, however, once again my problems don't seem bad at all. For a long while, she had been in a fair bit of pain when out running and had been diagnosed with a severe form of arthritis in her knees. The medical profession has told her that she shouldn't be running at all. But Kirsten has the most amazingly positive attitude, pushing herself to her limits and refusing to give up the thing that she loves and is central to her being. Just when she was managing the pain better, she was hit with some intense pain in her left foot that turned out to be three torn plantar plates. She told me that it felt like running on steak knives for hours on end.

Since surgery is unlikely to be successful, Kirsten has to work at shutting out, or at least trying to ignore, all the pain when she runs. With those handicaps she has run the Tahoe 200 (three hundred and thirty-one kilometres) and the Grand to Grand (two hundred and seventy-three kilometres), both major multi-day races in America. She's some tough cookie. When the pain gets too much, she simply turns up at events as a volunteer. Her cheerful outlook helps make the day for a lot of people. Folk like Kirsten keep me grounded and motivated.

One book I read recently talked about mindfulness in running and I have found that trying to adopt its approach, staying in the moment can be beneficial. I have to admit, however, that I find it extremely hard to keep it up for long. It's an ongoing fight that I continue to try and win.

In the depth of battle, as I shuffle along deep into a race, I sometimes wonder why I am doing this to myself. The pain can become excruciating and every step can feel like the next one will be impossible, even as I chant my mantra, 'I am strong, I run long.' The next aid station is perhaps miles away, it's pouring rain and I am facing a serious hill. The thought of many hours of struggling ahead of me can be torturous. In those situations, I find it easy to lose focus and feel sorry for myself. All I can see is the pain cave where I am huddled in a corner. Where does the strength come from to get to the finish line?

I know our late daughter Allison would tell me to just 'suck it up, old man'. At those times, I certainly find some kind of inner power when I think about her, as well as those who have supported me, like Dale, over the years, or all the people who have made donations to the causes I have run for. But deep down, below all the suffering, I know that all I can rely on is myself and the strength that my training has given me. After all, it's just a day (or more in some cases) out in the wilderness, so I focus on the fact that, like the mail in those old western movies, I will get through.

In the really bad times out on the trails, there's constant negative chatter in my head that is hard to ignore. 'That calf twinge is getting worse', or 'I don't think I'll finish' or even 'I might as well pull out now.' Especially in the middle of a long night on the trails when I am soaked through, shivering with the cold, 'Why am I putting myself through this when the family is all warmly wrapped up in bed asleep? I should be too. Come on, quit now and go home.' The endless babble of your mind can destroy all the good work you have put in up to then. In those difficult times, what you are hearing in your head does sound very sensible and attractive. But you need to recognise that disaster is heading your way if you keep listening to those negative conversations.

You have to turn it around quickly and start talking positively to yourself. I'm a little embarrassed to say, but I practise talking aloud in training. People I come across look at me strangely for sure, but it helps to dig me out of any hole I am sinking into. While I'm talking, there's no room for any incoming negative messages. Another mental trick that works for me is to find things to continually celebrate; anything – reaching the top of a hill, arriving at an aid station, even being told by another runner 'you're looking good'.

There's no doubt about it, the mental side plays a big part in ultra marathon running. Putting any tool, including mindfulness, in our mind's toolbox is going to help us get through those dark patches. And the more tools we have, the better we'll be able to deal with any challenge.

Running has taken me to some extraordinary places. Not just for organised events or even solo adventures. When my wife and I go on overseas holidays, I always pack my Hoka shoes and some running gear. It feels like a special treat when I head out of the hotels where we're staying. It's the best way of exploring a strange place that I know of, even if I have managed to get lost a couple of times.

In Singapore, I discovered a large park with a botanical garden near our hotel and it was a delight to run there in the early morning before the heat and humidity hit. A great way to run off the large but delicious dinner of the night before.

When we were in Egypt, I got to run up Mount Sinai in the dark and saw the sunrise over distant mountain ranges; so many steps to climb. Coming down was fast and exhilarating. Doing that in such a historic place was so uplifting.

While in India, staying overnight in a small town, I went out into the extreme heat and humidity just before dinner and enjoyed having a crowd of youngsters run alongside me. They laughed and wanted to practise their English, but we got faster and faster until we all stopped, breathless. Another evening in the same town, a man on a motor scooter slowed up beside me on a dirt road and kept asking if I wanted a lift. He was very puzzled to see someone running purely for pleasure– not a common sight in India I bet.

In England, I have run a fair part of the South Downs Way, which is a beautiful path through the countryside in Hampshire and Sussex. I had been staying at my mum and dad's house, but we all needed a bit of a break so I donned my running gear and headed off for two days. In bright sunlight, I ran out above the white chalk cliffs of Beachy Head on mind-blowing springy sheep-cropped turf, where I interrupted a crowd of birdwatchers lying on the ground with telescopes searching for a rare visiting bird. Hopefully, I didn't disturb them too much. Onwards along the cliffs, I could hear the waves crashing far below. Then it was on through some small villages with thatched cottages. I stopped at a small café for a bite to eat and a cup of coffee to recharge my batteries. My final leg took me into the seaside town of Brighton, where I stayed in a Youth Hostel overnight before heading back along the Way the next morning, feeling fully restored. Two days of running, stopping to smell the flowers and soaking up the scenery will do that.

Rarotonga in the Cook Islands was another interesting visit, but this time we went with a small group of runners from Flinders Island specifically for the Rarotonga Running Festival. Over three days, they held a variety of challenging events, but the main reason we were there was to run the Round Rarotonga Race. This is about a thirty-two-kilometre race through some really pretty scenery, but sadly that particular day it hammered down with rain, making it a hard run. Fortunately, the sun came out later so we could all enjoy a pleasant post-race lunch down by the ocean.

Dale and I had a romantic holiday on a minuscule island in the Pacific called Fafa, close to Tonga. There were only a handful of chalets circling the island, so very few people, which was perfect. Every morning before breakfast, I would go for my running fix – but it meant doing a giddy twenty laps around a trail carved through the coconut trees. I lost count several times but it never mattered.

Again, in Vanuatu, where we liked to go to escape the cold Tasmanian winters for a while, I would run for an hour every day through a village called Pango. My route took me past a school and a local football ground and then along the coast where local fishermen had set their fish traps and, eventually, via a quiet loop on a gravel road, back to our small resort. Stopping occasionally to talk to the locals, who were going about their daily village life, made an ordinary outing a bit special.

And I've always kept my eye open for the chance of spontaneous runs in places I haven't been before. I once got lost in the maze of tracks through King's Park in Perth. I hadn't been very watchful and it took ages to find my way out.

One time, on holiday in Vietnam, the small cruise ship that we were on in Hannalong Bay dropped us off on an island with a temple on top of the highest peak. I had no alternative but to don my Hokas and do several laps, up and down a long series of steps, even though it was typically very hot and humid – well, it beat lying on the beach and sunbaking.

Perhaps the greatest thrill, however, was the day I ran into the depths of the Grand Canyon in America. I passed many hikers from all parts of the world as well as two tourist groups riding donkeys. Going down was fast and fun, but it was exhausting coming back up in the extreme dry heat.

When I think of unusual runs I have had, the strangest must have been the day I ran with Yannis Kouros. I realise that sounds impressive, but the reality was somewhat different. It was, I think, the third Westfield Sydney to Melbourne race. Yannis had been given a twenty-four-hour handicap to give the other runners a fair chance.

Listening to the race news one evening in Sydney, a group of us decided that it would be cool to drive down to Canberra the next day and run a couple of hours with Yannis. We eventually found him a lot further on than we had expected. After leaving the car in a lay-by, we waited for him to come along. Yannis and his entourage were steaming along, having been running continuously for a day and night, plus the morning we arrived. When we saw him, it almost took our breath away. He was pure poetry in motion, moving so smoothly, like a well-oiled machine.

Anyway, with a loud shout of 'Aussie, Aussie, Aussie', we joined him on a dual carriageway somewhere on the city's outskirts. He didn't speak a word, remaining focused on his effort. Because Yannis made it all look so easy, I was a little shocked to find I couldn't keep up with him for more than half an hour. My legs were not used to turning over that quickly, I was sweating profusely and could feel my body overheating. Somewhat disheartened, I grunted farewell and turned back. What an incredible athlete he was, holding so many road and track ultra marathon world records it is ridiculous.

While I have enjoyed all the long stuff and especially the multi-day events, there have always been plenty of shorter fun runs to share with our integrated family and friends. Among my favourites is the annual Mother's Day Classic that takes place in Sydney's Botanical Gardens and raises funds for breast cancer research. Our whole family congregates there and runs in memory of our daughter Allison, who had encouraged us all to take part. As the years have passed, it's been a delight to see that not only are our children turning out and running good distances, the grandkids have also been getting into it. Such is the power of running.

16

Long May We Run

'Only those who will risk going too far can possibly find out how far they can go.' – T.S. Eliot

At the age of sixty-eight, I took on a running coach for the first time. I had heard a lot about Andy Dubois and his organisation, Mile 27, over the previous two or three years and, after chatting to him for a while on the telephone, I knew he could help me give the 2015 Big Red Run my best shot (although secretly I thought I needed something more like a small miracle).

I met Coach Andy a couple of times, initially to assess my running style/technique. We talked about his coaching process. It all sounded fine, apart from the tortuous strengthening exercise he was recommending I adopt. However, I committed to Andy's weekly emailed programme as if it were a religious text and, if it hadn't been for the terrible terrain in the Simpson Desert, I know I would have done better because of Andy's magic touch.

But since the 2015 event, I haven't felt the need for a coach. I'm not saying that I know all there is to know about training for ultras or any other race. I don't doubt that a coach would help improve my performances, but just having an adventure is now good enough for me. So I'm happy doing my own thing. It is clear, though, that in all walks of life, professional help can maximise our achievements.

My personal approach to training has always been one of using long, slow distance (LSD) as my bread and butter runs, with a day of hills and another of speed work. I prefer Fartlek out on my local bush trails, rather than speed work in the form of four-hundred-metre repeats or suchlike. I find Fartlek is a brilliant way of including speed into a training regime, as it's more fun and interesting than track work. I also find that I get fewer injuries from it. My personal Fartlek method is to pick out a tree or rock up ahead and decide at what pace I am going to run to it. On the shorter intervals, I tend to go as fast as I can, but sometimes I run for up to a kilometre at a fifty per cent extra effort. Once there, I shuffle along for a while, until my breathing has completely recovered, and then try for a different distance and speed. An hour of this work definitely employs the no pain, no gain philosophy.

LSD, though, is my principal training base. Apart from the fact that time on your feet is a sound platform to build on for long-distance races, I guess that I have always tremendously enjoyed the solitude of those long runs. It suits me to take it easy, soaking up the scenery around me or stopping to admire a view that I may have seen a thousand times before but which the light on a given day makes unique. I find the whole experience uplifting and, even though a morning's outing is definitely not the whole purpose of the day, it surely sets the tone for what that day will bring and how I can handle whatever it throws at me.

As my training gears up, I bring into effect the big guns – back-to-back long runs. The principle is simple, running the second day on tired legs. The distance covered on both days extends week by week and gives me a feeling of power and confidence in achieving my goals. Plus, these times are good for testing my eating and drinking habits. When I'm struggling later in a race somewhere, remembering those training back-to-backs keep me going forward, knowing that the strength is in my legs.

I have done these B2Bs out on the roads when getting ready for some of my charity runs but mostly they are best done on the trails around our island. I try to locate interesting loops that will bring me back to my ute at the end, rather than have my wife drive out to pick me up. As most of these trails have substantial hills in them, I really do have fatigued legs at the end of the first day and make the most of a good soak in a bath splashed with Radox.

Of course, for multi-day races I will even do back-to-back-to-back runs but only manage this once or twice. I think any more could cause injuries or bring on a cold or flu. Knowing what I am capable of at any time is the secret, rather than attempting too much too soon.

Plus, I enjoy a mandatory rest day once a week when I go for just a nice long power hike with the dog. Occasionally, I take my walking poles to keep my hand in, since I like to use them on difficult terrain in the multi-day events. When my training schedule is up near the sharp end before I taper for a race, and I am doing big back-to-back walk/runs as well as hills and speed work, I use a rest day as just that; a time to relax, do some reading or a little work in the vegie garden but nothing onerous. And it feels decadent.

At such a critical time in my training, taking a day off it makes me feel very guilty and I have to keep reminding myself that rest is essential to allow recovery for the hard work to come.

On some of those rest days, I feel strong enough to climb the highest of our local peaks, Mount Strzelecki (seven hundred and fifty metres). The track to the top is straightforward but there's plenty of rock-hopping to slow you up. There is a beautiful rainforest halfway up and a noisy creek flows most of the year. The record time for up and down is under an hour, which is amazingly fast, but it takes me around three with a few stops along the way to enjoy the view, eat and drink. The downward journey can have quite an effect on my knees, so I usually have a fairly easy run the following day.

In their pop hit single 'I Got You Babe', Sonny and Cher sing 'there ain't no hill or mountain we can't climb', and for many years I took this as one of my theme songs. I was always looking for new hills to tackle and add to my collection. I loved the challenge that hills gave, the satisfaction gained from as many exhausting repeats as I could manage. With sweat trickling into my eyes, I would stand with my hands on knees, gulping down air, knowing that even one more was beyond me. Unfortunately, since my bout of pneumonia in 2016 and the added concern of my more recent heart issues, I have had to forgo hill workouts.

One lesson I have learned the hard way in hill running is to never look up at the top; just concentrate on the few metres ahead of you. Time after time, however, especially when I'd been grinding it out, and my legs were full of lactic acid, with my heart pounding like some piece of ancient Victorian machinery, I couldn't stop myself. I knew that it would be suicidal to even take a quick squint up the hill – but then I would do it. Stupid, stupid. Immediately, my brain would tell my legs. 'That's it. Quit now and walk a bit. No harm done.' And you know, once you have conceded to the inner chatter of your mind, it is hard not to stop further on. Knowing you have already done so is a guarantee that you will permit yourself to walk again.

I was enjoying a chat with friends over a dinner of Atlantic salmon coated with Cajun spices, as well as a pleasant Chardonnay, when the subject of Ron Hill's running streak came up. As usual in these days of technological delights, someone quickly Googled it and we were all stunned to hear that Ron's history-making streak – during which he ran at least a mile every day – went for fifty-two years, thirty-nine days. Imagine that, never missing a day; even after surgery, he managed to go a mile on crutches. And I even recall a story of Ron shuffling up and down the aisle during a cross-Atlantic flight to keep the streak going.

Although Ron Hill had many great achievements in his illustrious career (he won the Boston marathon in 1970 and held world records in several distances), he is most widely known for that streak. I've known a few people who have got themselves caught up in a streak but it's something I have deliberately avoided like the plague. It seems to me that the streak has a life of its own and controls the runner, who lives in fear of it ending.

I can understand the obsession that drives a streaker and, somehow, admire people like Ron, but I've long recognised that my body must have rest days. And those days engender an increased desire to run afterwards. I wouldn't think that forcing yourself to run, even for a mile, when injured is going to do any good at all. So good luck to all budding Ron Hills – I'll applaud you from afar.

These days, I incorporate walking into my routine to, hopefully, put less stress on my body and give me extra running longevity. Having read Jeff Galloway's books on the subject some years ago, there is undoubted evidence to show that it works, even if it does mean I'll be slower than in my heyday. I use the run/walk method right from the word go at the start of every run as, otherwise, it doesn't work as effectively.

I have tried several different run/walk ratios. Some people like 8:2 but I prefer a shorter walking break to avoid my legs becoming stiff, so use a 4:1 ratio as my base. One minute seems long enough for me to have a drink or eat something light before shuffling off again. I use a small device called a Gymboss clipped to my waistband to tell me when to start and stop running, which allows me to easily change that ratio when required. This is a big advantage when I'm a few hours into an adventure and my mind decides to abandon ship and becomes incapable of any logical thought. Thankfully, the little Gymboss does the thinking for me. Anyway, it's a real pain to keep looking at a watch.

I have kept a handwritten running diary for many years and find it keeps me honest in my assessment of each run, but it's also useful looking back and seeing the result that each training period produced. Incidentally, for quite a while now I have only logged the time I have run plus, of course, the location, conditions and how I felt. I find that time is truer to my personal goals than distance. A lot of people I know get hung up on the distances they run each day. That's fine for them, but somehow I find it more restricting and sticking to time certainly avoids relying on the ubiquitous Garmin.

For timing purposes, I wear a simple Timex Ironman watch. I have had it for several years, changed straps several times and put in numerous new batteries, but it takes all that the weather throws at it and comes back strong every time. I can't remember how much it cost but it was dirt-cheap. I admit to having tried a Garmin for a while but prefer the simple approach of a Timex. I got sick of standing at the trailhead waiting for the Garmin to get a signal and then to find that it dropped out somewhere in the middle of my run. Frustrating, to say the least; plus, I didn't need to keep the data on my PC as I still preferred to write my daily log.

Everywhere I go on Flinders Island, the weather is the first topic of conversation, as I guess it is in any rural region across the world. 'How much rain did you get?' I am constantly being asked but, no matter how tough the conditions are on this little speck on Earth, we are blessed compared to those places that freeze over in winter (we get just a couple of frosts) or bake in their summers (we rarely go over thirty degrees), so trail running is my go-to most mornings.

But when it's pouring rain and blowing a gale simultaneously, I steer clear of the trails and head for our small local gymnasium. The local community worked very hard to obtain a grant from the Tasmanian Community Fund to build this space that has crisp white walls and a charcoal carpet. To date, we have only a few exercise machines but we are working on that. It is literally my port in a storm. The treadmill (aka 'dreadmill') is my principal focus and I get there early to stake my claim for a long workout. I dread spending an hour or two balanced precariously on a narrow moving belt, gazing forlornly out of the rain-spattered window, but I fight hard to remain as positive as possible.

One great suggestion to spice up a treadmill workout that I picked up somewhere is to take a pack of cards with me. The idea is that after warming up I have to pull any card out of the pack (ignoring the picture cards) and whatever number comes out, I move the gradient up for that number of minutes before returning to my regular elevation for the same time. I have found that this randomness takes away some of the boredom. And, of course, rock music or podcasts on my little iPod always help.

As I have mentioned elsewhere, we are all, as George Sheehan said, an experiment of one and it's up to each of us to discover the best training routine for ourselves. Or we can go the other way and seek out a coach's help. Either way, a regular programme is a sure sign that we are making progress towards our running goals.

17

The Pain Cave

'If something hurts, just ignore it – something else will take its place soon enough.' – Old saying in ultra running

We've all heard the adage 'You're either injured, about to be injured or recovering from an injury'…well, I have been all three many times and sometimes all three at once.

Like every other runner, I have experienced a plethora of injuries and setbacks. I have accepted that most of them are a result of over-training and usually occur when I am feeling ten foot tall and bullet-proof. Unfortunately, there is an element of inevitability about it; as I get stronger and fitter running-wise, I find it extremely difficult *not* to overdo things. The temptation is to do just a little bit extra and that so often proves to be my downfall. I retain the hope that I will eventually learn, but history has shown that I shouldn't raise my expectations.

Apart from the Big Red Run blister episode, the biggest 'suffer fest' I can remember was the 2017 Gone Nuts fifty-kilometre race in northern Tasmania. A week before the event, after training very well for four months, I lifted a twenty-litre petrol container a bit awkwardly and, bang, I put my back out. A bulging disc was diagnosed. I couldn't even stand straight for two days. Our local physiotherapist worked on me every day, I swallowed a pharmacy full of anti-inflammatories (the drug Ibuprofen is known by runners worldwide as 'vitamin I') as well as a variety of painkillers.

Even then, I knew that the doctor (yes, the same one who told me to stick to shorter races.) would tell me to cancel my entry as I was still in real pain. On the Richter scale, it was about 7 out of 10. So I wasn't going to make an appointment to see him as, of course, I already knew that it would be idiotic to run at all, let alone fifty kilometre through some pretty rugged country. But I'd paid the large entry fee, was booked to share a hotel room with a good mate and there was a group of islanders flying across to mainland Tassie for the event. It was going to be loads of fun; so, sure, I wasn't going to miss out.

Big mistake. I hadn't tried running at all during the previous week in an effort to give my back the best chance of recovering, but a mere ten minutes into the fifty-kilometre race, I knew I was in serious trouble. I broke into a very gentle shuffle as often as I could but was forced to walk again quite quickly. If you've seen the YouTube video of the racecourse, you'll know that it's in a really pretty but tough part of the Tasmanian countryside. Fortunately, the weather conditions were favourable, but everything else was against me. I even slipped on some tussock grass cuttings as I was going down a steep slope, fell on my bum and gave the problem disc another terrible jolt.

With the increased pain, I struggled to get to the twenty-five-kilometre aid station - but I did eventually and, after collapsing into a chair for five minutes, knew that I'd be crazy to continue. Another three or more hours of this was incomprehensible. All I wanted was to have a cold drink, lie down and let oblivion take over.

In desperation, I asked if there was a doctor around who could prescribe me some strong painkillers. I imagined being given a wonder drug that could get me running well to the finish line. Unfortunately, I was told it would be an hour before anyone could get to see me. As I sat there sinking into a dark abyss of despair and self-pity, I remembered the real suffering our daughter Allison had experienced over the last two or three years of her too-short life. I knew I couldn't let this pain beat me. I had no choice but to get back out onto the trail and to put one foot in front of the other, do that again and again and again and see what happened further down the track. No surrender.

Sure enough, I remained in constant back pain climbing up rocky ravines hanging on to bushes and small trees as my feet slipped and slid from under me. I could only accept that it was not going to get any worse. I was desperate to finish but it seemed so far away. Refusing to look at my watch, I knew I had to keep positive thoughts in my head if I was to get there. I pictured my loved ones, imagined myself crossing the finish line and chanted my usual running mantra 'I am strong, I run long' in time with my footsteps, blocking out any other thoughts. I power hiked and jogged in alternate short spells and, as it always must, the end came closer and closer – I could even smell the sausages cooking on the barbecue at the finish line and hear the beer cans popping.

As a measure of how well such a positive approach can succeed, I would say that I felt quite a bit stronger towards the end (a few Panadol might have helped) and even raced a couple of young ladies down the last kilometre to the finish. We laughed and laughed as we crossed the line and collapsed onto the grass completely spent. And just to let you know how hard that race was, the medical tent at the finish was packed with the wounded. Loads of runners were walking around with slings or bandaged parts as badges of courage.

I was very careful over the next couple of weeks to give my back as much rest as possible, with plenty of stretching and physiotherapy. Rather than attempting to run too soon, I regularly headed to the gym for some cross training.

Another 'injury' I suffered badly from was at the 2015 Convicts and Wenches fifty-kilometre race. This is an interesting out-and-backer, again held in northern Tasmania, where runners enjoy twenty-five kilometres along beaches of firm, wet sand with four headlands, covered in gnarly bush, separating those beaches before turning round. It was a nice hot day with a cloudless sky and a hint of a sea breeze coming in from the ocean, which lazily rolled in from the unusually peaceful Bass Strait.

I had been trotting along pretty well for the first thirty or so kilometres, enjoying life, and had just finished a long beach section. I was even looking forward to the last section of bush when it hit me. All I did was to raise my right leg a little higher to climb onto a step and my hamstring seized with a horrendous cramp. I collapsed to the ground and lay there, writhing in agony, for what seemed like ages until a runner coming up behind me helped me upright. From then on, I was forced to shuffle along like one of those terrorist prisoners you see on American TV with shackles on their ankles. Even so, I got debilitating cramps again several times and learned a huge lesson: never run fifty-kilometres the day after having had a colonoscopy. It turned out I was quite severely dehydrated before the race had even begun. A really stupid thing to do.

I have never been an active or regular stretcher. I have read opposing views on the subject and I only do so when it will aid an injury recovery process. Over the years, I have suffered from a bad back; slipped disc and sciatica – that sort of debilitating injury – which, funnily enough, I tend to incur when I'm pickaxing, wood splitting or chainsawing, rather than running. Those particular injuries stall my training for some time and I certainly incorporate regular and intense stretches every day until I'm fully recovered. But when I am 'normal', my warm-up consists of walking for the first couple of minutes, to give my legs a chance to understand what's expected of them, before the planned run/walk session begins.

Nor do I 'warm down' either. I usually remain fairly active throughout my normal days with plenty of walking and outside activities that seem to work fine. I know some people swear by pre- and post-exercise stretching, and if it works for them, then obviously I think it's the right thing, but I just don't seem to need it. After races, I have sometimes stretched hamstrings, quads and calves but tend to get some compression tights on as soon as possible, which helps as good as anything.

I believe that the best way to avoid an injury is to treat my body as kindly as possible. This certainly involves not pushing too hard over a long period, but I also try to have regular physio work done, as well as massages when I can get them. Living on a remote island, it is sometimes difficult to find such support but we are blessed with having a wonderful physio and fellow runner, David Heap ('Compost' to his mates), who keeps me in one piece and out there on the trails. It's great to get expert advice from someone who understands running and runners' needs.

So many people of my age that I see around have high cholesterol, type 2 diabetes or even major heart issues. They are on a plethora of drugs that further restrict their ability to be active. I am no expert and can't say definitely, but from what I have read and seen, turning to exercise later in life can help control some of the bad things that we have done to our bodies over the years. Of course, it would be better to become active before any such problems arise.

Recently on Flinders Island, David Heap and I started a Saturday morning park-run event, which has proved very popular with a wide range of ages. It is abundantly clear that several of our older regulars have taken up power hiking/walking to avoid the diseases that a sedentary lifestyle can bring in our senior years. And, certainly, they are finding such regular exercise beneficial. For many participants, park-run is their first experience of being in a timed event and it is lovely to see so many smiling faces as they challenge their previous best time.

It's also interesting to see an increasing number of senior people going to our local gymnasium and working at a routine tailored for them individually. It's just great that others of my vintage are committed to looking after their health. Long may they stay fit and injury-free.

18

Food For Thought

'We are all an experiment of one.' – George Sheehan

I heard the loud music before I saw anything. 'Barb, Barb, Barb – Barb Barb Barbara Anne, you got me rockin' an' a reelin'…' Suddenly, I came through a gap in some trees into the aid station, totally drained, not an ounce of energy left in my legs. All that held me up were my hiking poles. My stomach hadn't felt right for a couple of hours, so I hadn't been able put anything in it without chucking up. With my nutrition plan completely stuffed up, I had to find something that would bring me back from the brink.

Ignoring the old adage 'Beware the Chair', I collapsed into the nearest one and tried to pull myself together. A volunteer, sporting a long-haired wig and dressed in loud-coloured surfing gear, offered to help, but right then I couldn't verbalise exactly what I wanted. After sitting for a while, my gut seemed to settle and, if I was to continue, I had to get some food and drink inside me. The sugar in half a can of Coke cleared my head and I could focus on my original race plan. I had made a big mistake in nutrition intake but I hoped it wasn't too late. Some hot soup from the volunteers, who were singing along to the Beach Boys' music blaring from two speakers, and an energy bar from my backpack, went down well. I grabbed a couple of salted potatoes as I finished the Coke. Eventually, I was able to push myself back into the race.

But that mistake highlighted for me the critical importance of getting hydration and nutrition right, from the word go. Managing food and drink is a critical part of the strategy of running an ultra marathon.

You can get by in shorter races with a more relaxed approach, but ultras will lay bare any flaw or weakness you show.

In my search for answers, I found many in the book *Endurance Sport Nutrition* by Suzanne Eberle, that explained everything clearly. It took me quite a bit of trial and error before I could settle on a formula that worked for me. While that doesn't qualify me to give advice on these matters, I hope my experiences will give you some help in developing your own strategies.

Firstly, things have changed tremendously over the century that I have been running. From the consumption of sugar-loaded items in my early races, I think I now have a much more balanced approach to the subject – even though mistakes can still happen. Of course, there has been quite a revolution in the scientific development of specialist products that help no end, but we still have to discover what is right for each of us. To some extent, the opposite now holds true – we are spoiled for choice; we are constantly bombarded by extravagant claims in advertisements and emails. It's just a matter of experimenting.

I also discovered that I needed to think more about my eating habits generally. When I was training for my first twenty-four-hour track race, I found that my digestive system didn't handle meat too well, so I experimented with vegetarianism.

Many years later, I am what someone once described as being a 'vege-quarian', meaning that I eat seafood but no chicken or red meat at all. This diet (if you want to call it such) doesn't leave me feeling so bloated after a meal, but it does require a bit more effort in working out how to get protein three times a day. A friend of mine on Flinders Island, Bill Riddle, said to me when we first met, 'So, David, I hear you're a vegetarian…you must love lettuce.' Well, thank goodness it's a lot better than just rabbit food.

I have consciously worked hard at growing my own vegetables and, with the help of my good friend Spud Murphy, have built a large covered vegie plot after a plethora of possums devoured a whole bed of ripened broccoli overnight. Happily, this area provides us with a large variety of fresh organic vegies that we only need to supplement a little with purchases from our local supermarket. It gives me a lot a pleasure to work in the garden and satisfaction to be able to put such fresh and healthy produce on our plates every day. I grow enough summer varieties to be able to freeze produce for our winter consumption, minimising the purchase of vegetables flown in from distant lands.

Another wonderful thing about living on Flinders Island is the choice of seafood available. I am fortunate in being able to go out fishing in Spud's boat occasionally, when we catch plenty of flathead (the best eating fish I've come across), flake (gummy shark) or whiting. A good catch means that I can freeze quite a few meals to last Dale and me for a while.

But the question of food required specifically for running is a vexed one. Perhaps the most common quandary is what to eat before, during and after a training run or race. I am certainly not qualified to provide a scientific answer to that. Once again, there is no fits one, fits all solution – all I can tell you is what I have found works best for me.

Before a run

Bearing in mind most of my runs are early in the morning, I usually don't eat anything before heading out for an hour or so, just a cup of coffee to kick start me. If I'm going for a longer run/walk, especially in the winter months, I'll have a bowl of porridge or some toast, thickly spread with peanut butter. I make sure that this is at least an hour before I run. But deep down I know that an empty stomach works the best for my everyday runs.

During a training run

This is the hard bit that I constantly struggle with. Over the years, I have tried many commercial products and now have a personal preference for one kind of gel, one kind of energy bar and a specific drink containing carbohydrates and electrolytes. We experiment and find our own favourites.

If at all possible, I also like to have some 'real' food in my backpack on the really long runs, such as bananas, dates or salted nuts as a savoury alternative. Too much sweet food can be hard to consume after a couple of hours of running.

After a run

Immediately after running, I find it hard to eat anything, but I recognise that I need to get some protein in pretty quickly to allow my muscles to recover properly. So, as soon as I can, I have a protein shake of some sort, preferably using a high-quality protein powder.

Thinking about how I handled nutrition in races, I recall a funny but frustrating incident that happened to me in the 2014 Bruny Island (a lovely rural retreat just outside of Hobart) Ultra. This is a great event that incorporates relay teams, as well as individuals running the sixty-four kilometres from one end of the island to the other. Most runners have a support crew in a vehicle along the roads to provide their needs. In a brave attempt to gain some sort of brownie points, I thought it best not to impose on Dale again and would run the event 'bareback'. So, choosing a simple diet of bananas and water, I placed a cache every ten kilometres along the road, with a special treat/pick-me-up of a bottle of Coke planted strategically about ten kilometres from the finish line, which is at a lighthouse sitting at the top of a long flight of steps, when I knew the going would get tough. That last section is on badly maintained gravel roads with corrugations so big that the local wallabies sleep in their shadows.

My nutrition plan was shot to pieces from the word go. The start of the run went smoothly enough, through some lovely hilly countryside with little traffic, but when I got to my first cache, I found that a possum had eaten my banana – even the skin; just the plastic bag was left behind. Damn it, but at least I had more up my sleeve, so to speak, further along the road. No I didn't. They had all been stolen, presumably by different possums. But for a moment I did imagine a long-distance running possum somewhere ahead of me collecting every one, with a huge smile on its face.

Worse was to follow. As usual in these long-distance runs, my brain turned to a mushy soup after a few hours, incapable of clear or even decisive thoughts. It was as if it had gone to live somewhere else, but hadn't bothered to let me know. So, when I had run over fifty kilometres and got to the place where I thought that I had put the bottle of Coke, I couldn't find it. It was meant to be behind a big gum tree that I had carefully selected. When I got there, I found that all the trees looked the same. I shuffled up and down the road, for what seemed like ages, searching behind every one without success. The trouble was (1) it was very warm; (2) I was in desperate need of fluids; (3) I was now in a bad place mentally, couldn't think clearly at all; and (4) I was in a fair amount of leg pain.

As always, however, I got over the blue funk, gave up looking and concentrated on putting one foot in front of the other and reciting my usual rhythmic mantra 'I am strong; I run long' until the final, desperately steep climb to the lighthouse door which marks the end of the race. Fortunately, as there were no aid stations provided in this race, some very generous relay runners came to my rescue, letting me have some of their water as they loped past.

So it's now clear to me that, apart from never trusting possums, I need to make sure that I mark clearly where I have put any stash of food or drink in such circumstances. I also know that I must use properly sealed plastic containers if I am to keep my nutrition safe from the local wildlife.

Racing

In the lead-up to a race, I adopt a different approach. Through trial and error, I have found my gastrointestinal system prefers lighter but more frequent meals the day before the event. And it seems that I perform better if I increase carbohydrate intake (nothing so technical as proper 'carbohydrate loading', though) the day before.

Racing is another issue. All the training helps get your body and mind prepared but the real test is race day. The food and drink consumed is critical to a good performance. There is an old saying that an ultra marathon is not a race but an eating competition. The body needs to consume regular amounts of carbohydrates to replace depleted glycogen stores, but how much and how often are things we can only discover by trial and error. The maxim of 'eat before you're hungry and drink before you're thirsty' is a good one to follow. It takes time for anything you put down your throat to be absorbed. If I leave it too long before eating and drinking, I get into all sorts of trouble.

It's been interesting to learn what my body wants on any given race day. It constantly changes, so I try to make sure that I have interesting alternatives in my backpack for later in the event – especially real food. There's nothing worse than feeling like you don't fancy eating anything you've got with you. And sugary food can suddenly become very unappealing.

For multi-day events, planning exactly what food and drink you are going to use is critical. Obviously, it's important to calculate both the weight and calories as the restrictions placed by the race organisers are strictly observed.

I just hope that the choices I have made in training will be the right ones, and that the food and drink I have taken will be enough to combat the accumulating fatigue over the course of the event.

Equipment

As I have already guiltily admitted, buying running 'stuff' is one of my major delights. Looking for the right things occupies quite a bit of my time. The trouble is that all running magazines, podcasts and videos loudly promote the appeal of every shoe, backpack, rain jacket, headlamp and every other imaginable product that us runners could ever desire or dream about. It takes an awful lot of willpower to ignore a full-page advertisement of anything, especially if there is a picture of a runner flying through some amazing snow-capped mountain country.

Obviously, good gear is critical in helping produce the best race result but, of course, we need only a pair of old shorts and some sneakers to actually be able to run. I totally acknowledge that running at its basic level requires very little in the way of equipment but, when you are perhaps a little bit obsessive about it and you become keen to improve, it's impossible not to look at anything that may help.

In my love of multi-day running, I have found it necessary to use high-quality gear. The last thing you want is for your equipment to fail during a long race. For instance, my backpack has to provide easy access to drinking bottles as well as gels and energy bars and so on. If you have to keep stopping and taking the pack off to access things, it becomes a nuisance and wastes critical time. Sure, cheap packs are available but, considering how important it is and how long you will be wearing it in training as well as racing, I would argue that the top end of the market is the only way to go. The backpack I have has done its job well for a few years now so, in my book, it was money well spent.

Similarly with winter gear, head torches, shoes and every other item you can think of. Good-quality stuff will last a lot longer. I once bought a pair of cheaper running tights for cold conditions but it only lasted for one season and seemed to stretch and become loose, not doing the job it was meant to. So, in effect, it was a waste of money. I had to buy a decent pair the next winter.

Probably the biggest conundrum every runner faces is what shoes to buy. Naturally, we all become hesitant to change the shoes that seem to suit us and the running stores and Internet don't allow us to try new ones out before purchase. And good shoes are expensive, so naturally we hesitate to experiment.

In recent years, a lot of research has gone into the technology of shoe design, especially the foam used to provide the best cushioning while ensuring that the shoe is as light as possible. Finding the right balance between weight and cushioning is tricky for anyone and when you look at the information available on the Web, it's hard to sort the wheat from the chaff.

A few years ago, as a result of Chris MacDougall's book *Born To Run*, barefoot running became popular worldwide. It was claimed that our bodies were designed to run without shoes, which made sense. Since I wasn't up to running barefoot on rocky and rugged trails, I went for the nearest alternative. I bought a pair of minimalist shoes with zero-drop soles and ran short distances in them for a couple of weeks. But I quickly realised that they didn't suit my running style at all. My body needed a lot more cushioning, especially for ultra marathons, so I reverted to the Hoka brand that I had been using for a long time. As long as they produce highly cushioned shoes with good toe space, I don't think I will change. They say you can't teach an old dog new tricks – and in this old dog's case they're right.

19

A Time to Learn

'If you get to be one hundred you've got it made – very few people die past that age.' – George Burns

Does wisdom come with old age? No chance.

When I listen to runners after a race as we lay on the grass completely spent, I often hear 'Well, I learned something from the mistake I made in that run. I won't be doing it again, that's for sure.' Right…

I don't know if it's only me, but I tend to make the same mistakes time after time, even though I assure myself that I won't. Maybe I'm incredibly dumb but I do know that, as I have mentioned, my brain becomes fried later in a long event and I am incapable of remembering *anything*, let alone what happened in a similar situation previously.

Take for example the definitive rule against doing anything in a race that you haven't tried in training. A pretty standard and sensible rule, I'd say. Although my eating habit in training and early in races is well established and I am very happy to get through on my chosen nutrition, things change when I shuffle into an aid station late in a long race, feeling desperately tired and sometimes pretty miserable to boot. Then watch out. I'm looking for any miracle that might be going and I'll grab all sorts of things on the table that look great; maybe some watermelon, potato chips, pretzels and, oh, what about a slice of pizza – it all goes down easily enough and I walk out of the aid station getting ready to break into my awesome (I told you my brain gets mushy, so right then I believe it's awesome) shuffle. About fifteen minutes later, my stomach rebels against it all and I either burp miserably for hours or just bring it all up in a bush somewhere along the trail. Now, while I've sworn not to do such a stupid thing again, at the very next race I enter, there appears to be the ideal food sitting on the aid station table with my name written all over it. I know how ridiculous this sounds in the cold light of not running, but I can't seem to help myself when I get in that situation.

Another thing I used to be guilty of was starting a race too fast. Everyone told me, 'You'll burn out too early if you can't make yourself go slow for the first few kilometres.' As clearly as night follows day, I knew this was true, but in the excitement of the moment I had been known to jump (relatively speaking.) out of the starting blocks, believing that it was my day and I'd be able to run a vast distance faster than I ever had before. At that moment, it felt like I was unbreakable but reality soon crept back in and I had to adjust my pacing if I was to survive to the end.

One of the best examples I saw of pacing came from my old Tassie mate Kim Denwer in the 2015 Big Red Run. Every day in the cool, crisp early morning, he started slowly, right at the back of the field, chatting to everyone and then gradually moving up to the next group, more chat and then on again. Each day, he had bonded well with most of the runners on the course, finished strongly and was fit for the next day. I wish I could do that.

It was sometime in the 1980s that I almost died in a race and I wasn't even running.

I had received a phone call from a friend who told me that a catamaran entered in the MMI 3 Ports Race was short of a runner. The race was a sailing event stopping at three spots on the New South Wales coast, where the runners would go ashore and complete a run through the bush before returning to their boat and heading off to the next venue. I'd never done such a race and was a little apprehensive about being at sea in a small boat overnight but, what the heck, it was another adventure outside of my comfort zone, and so I was in.

The three legs of the running sections went well; I was nowhere near the sharp end of any of them but, as always, enjoyed the company of other runners and being out there in the beautiful Aussie bush. Things changed, however, when I boarded the catamaran to sail north for the final leg of the event.

The idea was that we would turn round at Lion Island, somewhere near Newcastle, and head back southwards to the finish in Middle Harbour (Sydney). I had just eaten some reheated pasta down in the cabin and was feeling a little queasy, so I went up on deck for air. It was pitch black on a moonless night as we neared the furthest point north. The crew was resting on deck with a rum and Coke when I happened to ask, 'What's that white water ahead?' All hell broke loose and it became clear that the sailors hadn't looked at their charts in detail. We were heading straight for a reef over which large white-crested waves were breaking.

The drinks were chucked overboard and the captain made the instant and courageous decision to go over the reef under full sail. We all hung on for grim death and I held my breath for what seemed like an eternity, as we roller coasted over the rocks lying just below the surface. Scary stuff indeed, but we made it unharmed. As you can imagine, all I wanted was to get back on dry land. I'll never mix running and sailing again – a salutary lesson that I did learn.

I also recognise the absolute power of preparation in running and, indeed, in all parts of life. We have all entered races having done insufficient training for one reason or another. I have been as guilty of it as the next person. A cold or minor injury or even, heaven forbid, something in the non-running part of our world, can interfere with the best-laid plans, but we decide to run the scheduled event anyway. And fair enough, I say; it's better than missing out altogether.

But how much better is it to be fully ready, not just having the appropriate training under our belt, but making sure all the race gear is fully functional; do we have spare batteries for our head torch, are the water bottles and bladder clean, have I got the proper blister kit including a sterilised needle? To minimise any stuff-ups, I go through a detailed written checklist, as I'm packing or repacking or even re-repacking for the umpteenth time.

There's nothing more frustrating than experiencing failure of one piece of equipment or another when you need it. I learned pretty early on that I should take spares of whatever essentials I can fit into my backpack, especially a substitute head torch and spare batteries if the race is likely to go into the night. Losing the ability to see on a bush trail in the middle of a moonless night makes running and navigation impossible. When this once happened to me, because of flat batteries, I was fortunate in being able to shuffle along behind another runner, but I still fell a couple of times and felt out of control. Never again will I be so ill prepared, I can assure you. It only has to happen to you once.

The briefings before a race can provide critical information and, occasionally, in the bigger crowds of runners I have been unable to hear some of the detailed instructions given. Through experience, I have found it best to ask a fellow runner or the race director to repeat the unheard bit; they don't mind. When you're totally alone out in the wilderness and you start to worry that you've gone the wrong way, it's important to know that you haven't missed some route change mentioned at the start. There's enough to worry about without those sorts of fears.

No matter what a race/event costs it is worth it. I am certainly not so well pocketed that money matters can be ignored, but I have found, time and time again, that I can scrimp and save to find a way to enter an event, or even to organise a fund-raising run. That's a part of the overall challenge: part of the preparation for it all, so to speak. But here's the thing – a year later and I've forgotten all about how much something had cost and how hard it was to raise the money. It is the memory of the event that remains forever imprinted in my mind. And, to be honest, that is all that matters when everything is said and done.

I read in one of my many running books that taking part in a marathon or ultra shows us that what we had first thought impossible becomes possible. I have found that to be true, but it cannot happen without commitment, hard work, dedication and prioritisation. Simply dreaming or hoping isn't going to cut the mustard. It is also truly said that the actual running of an event is just the celebration of all the hard work that has gone into the training beforehand. It is OK to be in awe of your own achievements and to acknowledge to yourself a job well done.

The relationship between the body, the mind and the governing brain is an interesting one from an ultra runner's perspective. Somewhere I heard a debate on exercise where it was claimed that what our body experiences affects the way our mind deals with all of life's issues. The more I think about this, the surer I am that it is true. The person talking was referring to mountain climbers but it is also pertinent to runners. If I had not been a lifetime runner, I doubt whether I could have dealt so calmly with many of the setbacks that life has thrown in my path. That isn't to say that I am not upset by personal tragedies or issues, but rather that I have managed them better than I think I would have otherwise.

On the other hand, of course, it's the brain that controls the body's movements and, in times when extreme exhaustion hits us during a tough event, the brain wants to protect us by trying to shut the body down and take us out of the race. It is only the strength of the mind that can overcome the brain's demands in those situations.

It's amazing how this body, brain and mind trilogy is balanced by a runner's understanding of him or herself. We don't come to terms with such a complex relationship easily, but hours on our own out on the trails will certainly help to make us stronger in every department.

When you first change your life in a positive way such as becoming a regular runner, I am sure that, like me, you will notice the effect it has on the people around you. Even those closest to you can feel uncomfortable with your choices and sometimes that can be challenging to deal with. But things change and what had been seen as unusual behaviour will become seen as the new normal.

When Flinders Island first became our home, it was a carnivore's delight. On an island famous for its milk-fed lamb and (my wife's favourite) Cape Grim beef, it was difficult to find vegetarian dishes at all. Even the potato salads at social barbecues had bacon in them. The tables would be groaning under the weight of all the chops, steaks, sausages, chicken and other meaty delights, but all beyond my 'vegequarian' reach.

I remember going into our local café and asking for a bowl of the vegetable soup that was on their menu, only to find that it had 'just a bit of ham in it'.

Since those early days on Flinders, however, things have changed quite dramatically. At barbecues, I can now find vegie burgers sizzling away, while the Sports Club (who have been among the biggest supporters of my fund-raising runs) even cook me fish at their functions. I guess they reckon I need feeding up.

Finally, the greatest lesson of all is one that makes me humble. Very humble indeed. Over all the years and all the events I have run, the thing that stands out the most is the family of runners that I have been adopted by. Many times I have arrived at a race knowing not a soul but by the time I am packing my gear away and heading to the car, train or airport, I am part of an increasingly large and very supportive family. It's great that we can stay in touch via the modern social network, but that is only a small part of this special worldwide group of people. Reach out for help and you'll be surprised at the responses. Need someone to run with tomorrow morning? What about travelling to a far off race alone? Does anyone know about how to prevent blisters? Countless questions, a countless number of running friends will be there for you with suggestions and support. And the unbelievable lifetime friendships made along the way? Priceless.

20

Hanging in There

'I hope I can always desire more than I can accomplish.' – Michelangelo Buonarroti

I was fifty-two when I was diagnosed with bowel cancer. The specialist couldn't believe that a man my age, who ran ultras and was a vegetarian, could contract this disease, but cancer does not discriminate. I was lucky, though; I had a great surgeon, who told me we had caught it early and, although it would take time for my body to recover, it should do so fully, which was far more fortunate than our lovely young daughter Allison, who had succumbed to this dreadful disease at the age of twenty-eight after a courageous battle.

It took a long time before the massive scar on my abdomen had healed (these days, it's a less intrusive operation, I believe) but after a few hiccups, I was back to my old self. Mind you, to this day, having only half a bowel does have some effect on my digestive system's behaviour. But, more importantly, the operation gave me food for thought. It forced me to realise what was important in my life. I guess that everyone who has had such a wake-up call says the same thing and it's a shame that it has to take such a traumatic and soul-shaking event to make us appreciate what is important. I already knew how important Dale and our new integrated family were, but I became more sharply aware that I had to make the most of each and every day. Before that, I had, I reckoned, just drifted along, going with the flow but not really 'enjoying the moment'. Now I was determined to do precisely that.

In order to maximise the enjoyment of my everyday life, I needed to get as fit as I could be and use that fitness once again to push myself to find what I was capable of being. I recalled how much I had loved running generally and running ultras in particular, but I had been foiled in my earlier attempts to get back to anything resembling running. It wasn't until we moved to Flinders Island that I was able to start again properly.

If ultra marathons were easy and pain-free, I doubt if anyone would want to run them. It seems to me that runners in such events are in them to prove to themselves that they can overcome the pain and adversity and through such transcendence feel truly alive. If that sounds a trifle trite, I would quickly point out that many of the runners I have spoken to have to a man (and woman) agreed that it is because the races are tough, painful and require long, arduous training that they are a true challenge, and it is that challenge within themselves that they love.

Running five kilometres is an achievement on its own, but once you've run a few five-kilometre races, most people naturally start to look for a new challenge. Maybe ten clicks, a half marathon or even a triathlon. Whatever it is that floats your boat, you sure as hell have to go for it. Underneath, we're all proud of our own running level, and rightly so. It's a bit like belonging to a secret society; we have a certain kind of uniform and meet in the strangest of places. Sometimes, our meetings (workouts or races) are over before the rest of the world has woken up and we are home, showered and getting on with our day full of energy. Nobody else has any idea of what we have done.

It's an absolute delight when we meet a like-minded spirit and sometimes it is people we would have least expected to have something in common with. I used to have regular meetings with a high-powered accountant, where we discussed mutual clients' affairs, but he remained distant to me for several years until one day I met him out running. After discovering that he was keen to run his first marathon, I did some training runs with him and we agreed to run the 1984 Sydney Marathon together. Unfortunately, he suffered terrible cramping in the second half of the event and it was over five hours before we struggled across the finish line. But it was something we always had in common and at every subsequent meeting we chatted about our mutual addiction before anything was said about business. We went to each other's houses and became good friends. All this because of a healthy passion for running.

Sure, today I struggle with being an OFR. I'm slower than I'd like, it takes longer to recover from races and injuries, and I struggle with arthritic pain but, hey, everyone can tell a similar story. Being older might slow you down but it shouldn't stop you. It is just another challenge to overcome. Who wants to wake up in the morning and spring out of bed without a twinge or care? If that happened to me tomorrow, I would be worried there was something seriously wrong.

My running life has taken me to many heights and a few lows, but I have always had my eye on the Dees that can creep up on me or any runner.

Demented, Deranged? This is what many people tend to call me when they learn what it is that turns me on. Or am I simply a Desperado who is Devastated, Depressed or Destroyed after a more than tough adventure? In fact, the Dees are none of the above – rather, I'm thinking of the worst possible things that can happen to me out on trail races, namely 'Did Not Finish' (DNF) or even the very worst, DNS – 'Did Not Start'.

From a certain perspective, DNF is the most soul-destroying result that can happen to a runner. People I've run with have gone through sheer hell and high water for hours at a time, only to find that they reach a point when their body shuts down, they just can't continue and are forced to pull out somewhere near the finish. This can happen for a smorgasbord of reasons: gastrointestinal issues, dehydration, damaged muscles or just plain old total exhaustion, where one more step is impossible – the list goes on. It is devastating when it happens. but I have been incredibly fortunate to avoid such a disaster in any race I have started.

Much as I suffered in a lot of my races, I have always been able to force myself to the end. There have been many times when I didn't think I could get there, but sheer bloody-mindedness, determination and support from runners and volunteers have pulled or pushed me to drag my body across the line. Mind you, it probably looked pretty ugly and I might have been wiser to pull out of a couple.

The nearest that I ever got to DNFing was in the 1983 Macao Marathon. I had run the Sydney Marathon two weeks before, but my legs felt recovered enough to convince me that I didn't need to train a great deal; just rock up and run it. That was my first mistake. The second and most critical error was to return to the scene of many a downfall, the Kowloon Cricket Club. The point was that I had returned to Hong Kong for a bit of a holiday and to see some of my friends who still lived and worked there. And where would I be most likely to see them all at the same time? The bar at the club, of course. So I joined them on their nightly celebrations over the few days before the race started, then caught the daily ferry across to Macao, an island about an hour's ferry ride from Hong Kong. In those days, Macao was mostly known for its casinos.

I felt a little seedy on the journey but, mistakenly, put this down to seasickness. I had a good night's sleep in a pretty crummy hotel (that had a twenty-four-hour casino on the ground floor), before dressing the next morning and walking in the darkness to the start line. If you have ever been to Hong Kong or, indeed, elsewhere in China, you will know the sharpness of some of the early morning smells and the incessant noise that assaults your ears, even in the hours when most sane people are asleep. At that stage, I had started to feel uncertain and perhaps a little nervous about the race, as I had no idea of what the course was like or what the day would hold. My head had cleared from the previous days' excesses, so all I had to worry about was my somewhat dodgy gastric region.

Leaving the hotel in the humid darkness to walk to the start line with a crowd of strangers was a little daunting, but I had to laugh when half of them disappeared – they were simply going home after a big night out at the casino.

When the gun sent us on our way, I shuffled along in a determined manner but felt distinctly out of sorts. I may not have had a hangover but my body didn't seem to know what was expected of it. It was going to be a long day. By the time I had reached thirty-five kilometres, and we had crossed the steepest bridge known to man, I was desperately tired and could only think about quitting. Every step hurt.

Just then, I came up to a man about my age who was running his first marathon. From what he said, he was suffering even more than I was. It was clear to both of us that we couldn't make it on our own, so we joined forces, encouraging each other all the way, somehow getting to the line together in just over four hours. A DNF had been a close call, averted by the kindness of a stranger.

So it's not the DNFs that concern me, but rather the fear of DNS (Did Not Start) that occupies my mind in the lead-up to any event. After obsessing for so long over every aspect of a race, as the big day approaches I become more and more nervous and a little irritable. Every twinge or ache in my body is cause for worry, mostly without reason. Although there was one particular time when I was truly knocked out of an adventure that I had been planning for ages. It was during an exciting road trip in the USA that had been planned to coincide with a fifty-kilometre race in Bryce Canyon National Park, Utah, which is quite amazing in its scenic beauty. The canyon itself sits on a high plateau and contains a large number of hoodoos (irregular columns of rock) left after erosion of the surrounding canyon of red, white and pink rock. A simple walk along the rim was enough to impress on us the wonder of the place.

Dale and I had been enjoying quite an adventurous trip experiencing some of the best desert places on offer, including the famous Death Valley that I will talk about later. Frustratingly, I had been suffering from a constant cough for quite a while and had been diagnosed with 'walking pneumonia' just two days before the Bryce Canyon run. I shouldn't have even thought about starting – but obsession is oblivious to reason. A large section of my suitcase was filled with gear for this run; it had been staring me in the face for the last two weeks and this was meant to be my big race of the year. There was no way I was going to miss out (or so I thought).

I collected my bib number and hastened out into the freezing early morning start. Being at high altitude, the cold dawns can still lead to very hot days. My hacking cough had started up again after a mostly sleepless night. At the start line, runners were huddled around a blazing wood fire rubbing their hands together waiting for the gun to go off. I joined them, trying not to cough too much but knowing what I was about to do was extremely stupid. From the start, I staggered along at the back of the field for less than two kilometres before a wave of coughing brought me to a standstill. The reality of the situation didn't take much working out. I turned around, walked back to our hire car and returned to our motel, well and truly chastened. As this happened so close to the start, I think it qualifies as a DNS rather than a DNF but, whatever it is, I had learned an invaluable lesson – accept that you can't start every event you register for. Shit happens.

You cannot plan for all the good and bad things that life is going to throw at you. Accepting them all as they are and reacting realistically to them, then moving on mindfully is something I have tried to do – not always successfully, mind you, but I continue to try.

The final Dee that confronts me in particular is the dreaded DFL (Dead F'ing Last). As an OFR I have seen myself getting slower and slower. I have refused to concede that some distances are beyond me but, despite keeping speed work in my training for as long as I could, Old Father Time has certainly put the brakes on me. So, for quite a few years, I have focused on making sure that I am not the last person to finish. I know that I am meant to think that at least I am taking part, but I can't help fighting the dreaded DFL. Perhaps it's the final goal I have to aim at. I was successful at this for a long time until I least expected it.

Back in 2012, I entered and ran a marathon in the small but pretty and very friendly seaside village of Penguin in northern Tasmania. The day had a few distance options and I could see we were all starting at the same time, with only a few registrations for the full marathon. It was a perfect day and I quickly settled into a pleasant rhythm for the first half, running and chatting to another competitor, but watching carefully to make sure that there was, indeed, always someone behind me wearing the marathon bib. At the halfway turn-round mark, however, a couple of people at the back of the pack dropped out unexpectedly. I could see that I was now last. Not to worry, though, as I could see a tall male runner a little ahead of me. I smiled inwardly, knowing that I had enough in my legs to catch and pass him nearer the finish, especially as he seemed to be struggling a bit. It was then that disaster struck.

Just as I caught him around the thirty-five-kilometre mark, the poor man collapsed in a heap on the road. Fortunately, it was right outside someone's house and we were able to call an ambulance straight away. As they drove off to the hospital (luckily it turned out that he was just dehydrated), I came to the cold, sobering realisation that I was firmly in last place. There was no one to be seen in front of me, so I just had to suck it up and cross the line Dead F'ing Last. And I have to admit it didn't feel as bad as I had thought it would (finishing never does) – it's just something I will continue to battle in the future.

21

Booked to Run

'After a life on the road, reading anchors me.' – Keith Richards

Looking through my open study door, I can see a collection of running books that I have accumulated over the years. Their colourful spines and strange titles always draw me towards that particular shelf. There are well over a hundred of them now and I have placed them at eye level: pride of place in my floor to ceiling library. They have such inspiring titles as *Duel in the Sun, My Year of Running Dangerously, Pole to Pole, Running on Empty* and even *Running Until You're 100*. They all bear witness to the authors' love of running and the desire to do something extraordinary.

I grew up devouring every book that I could get hold of. My parents weren't very keen readers, so I don't know where the addiction came from, but when I wasn't outdoors, my head was stuck in a book. After school, when cricket practice was finished, I would often cycle to the local town and scour the second-hand bookshops in the back streets. I didn't have much pocket money but what I had went on such classic adventure books as *Treasure Island* or *Robinson Crusoe*, stories that totally absorbed me.

Today, I remain a very keen second-hand book devotee. My wife and I search out bookshops wherever we go and always try to leave some space in our suitcases in case we strike gold. The first place I check out is the sports section and you'd be surprised by the number of old running titles that I have found there. I also use the Internet a fair bit to help feed my addiction but there's nothing quite like holding a book in your hand before you part with your money.

Books are a wonder; they can take you to places and give you vicarious experiences that you might never be able to have first hand. For example, a few books have been written about the Badwater 135 Race run across Death Valley in extraordinary temperatures across some of the most inhospitable terrain you'll ever find. One of them, *To The Edge* by Kirk Johnson, takes you right there; you can feel every sensation that he is feeling and almost get the sense that you are running right alongside of him. We should never underestimate the power of the written word.

The Internet is a wonderful tool for finding treasures. As soon as I read or hear somewhere about a running book that I haven't got on my shelf, I jump online and track down a good used copy or face up to it and buy a new copy. The website www.betterworldbooks.com has a huge range of great second-hand books at low prices, and better still they mail them free to anywhere in the world. This is particularly attractive when you live in Australia, as the postage from USA can be quite exorbitant. There's the added advantage of knowing that your purchases help Better World Books fund world literacy.

My all-time favourite running reads are *Ultra Marathon Man* by Dean Karnazes, *Born to Run* by Chris McDougall, and *Running and Being* by Dr George Sheehan.

All three of those books have been an inspiration to me and multiple readings don't detract from the power of their impact. Bill, a runner I came across, told me what a revelation it had been for him to read *Born To Run*. He had always had his daily run through the bush on his own and hadn't realised there were others out there doing the same thing until he discovered that book.

I would also recommend reading *Duel In the Sun* by John Brant. It's the thrilling story of the 1982 Boston Marathon, where the two leading runners, Alberto Salazar and Dick Beardsley, pushed themselves to their limits. The book is not just about the race itself, however, but what led up to it and what it did to both those wonderful athletes afterward. Salazar went into deep depression and Beardsley fell into felony drug addiction. The race cost them both dearly. The book is a real page-turner – don't miss it.

I also have a small collection of videos showing races in some wild places, including *Unbreakable*, *Running On the Sun* and *Desert Runners* – all well worthy of watching a few times.

Then, of course, there's my wonderful mind-boggling addiction to watching YouTube. It can certainly be a black hole if you let it and I have let it when I should have been attending to more important issues. Sometimes, I have spent an hour or two watching video clips of various ultra marathons that people like Killian Jornet have won or the Ginger Runner has filmed. There's so much good stuff out there, I don't want to miss anything exciting.

Fear of missing out (FOMO) applies to such behaviour as much as it does to running, when you can't stop yourself from entering too many races and become injured or mentally worn out. But where else can you find short video clips of ultra runner Anton Krupicka with his flowing hair and wearing just a pair of running shorts and old joggers, simply flying up a mountainside with the greatest grace imaginable? Where else can you find films of races that you are thinking of entering? Yes, YouTube holds a vital place in my online running library. I simply type in 'ultra marathons' and I'm sucked in for sure.

Podcasts are also an important part of my running armoury. They can be great company on a solo long run – just like having someone chatting alongside you. There's such a wide range of dedicated running podcasts but those I listen to regularly include *Find Your Feet, Running In the Centre of the Universe* (Ashland Dave has become a long-distance mate of mine over the years) and *Ginger Runner Live.*

When I'm ready for something non-running related, I tend to turn to true crime podcasts; my mind boggles at the terrible things people can do to each other. My favourite choice is *Casefile True Crime,* which looks at serious crimes committed across the world. The narrator is an Australian who tells the stories in an in-depth and interesting way.

There is also a large number of audiobooks available to download onto your devices. I have listened to quite a few on my multi-day adventures, including a couple of running books. Like podcasts, they help tremendously in keeping the mind away from dark pain cave thoughts.

22

The End of the Trail?

'Life should not be a journey to the grave with the intention of arriving safely in a pretty and well-preserved body, but rather to skid in broadside in a cloud of smoke, thoroughly used up, totally worn out and loudly proclaiming "Wow. What a ride."' – Hunter S. Thompson

Who knows what the future holds for any of us? I could never have predicted that I would have been here on this beautiful island for the last twenty years with my lovely wife. I certainly didn't think back when 'I wore a younger man's clothes' (as Billy Joel once sang) that I would be out there entering ultra marathons when I was seventy years plus.

While I sometimes optimistically believed that I was indestructible, in reality I understood that circumstances might arise when I could be forced to quit long-distance running, at any time for any number of reasons. Now that I have reached the point where I have to face the fact that stopping is a possibility, I do my utmost to stay positive and believe in my ability to keep on keeping on. I will still get out onto the local bush trails every day I can and continue to seek adventures in beautiful places. I refuse to lie down willingly.

You never know what life holds for you, though. One day you're fine and the next…gone. If you believe that there's something you want to do, just grab it straight away. Waiting can make you miss out. I believe (and I'm not the only one) that to live life to the limits you can't wait for anyone or anything. The ancient Roman poet Horace famously wrote, *'Carpe diem quom minimum credula postero,'* which I think translated roughly means 'Live for today with little regard for the future.' Nothing has changed in over two thousand years.

We are certainly not like the cans and packets on our kitchen shelves with use-by dates stamped on our backsides. We can set out to do whatever we want at whatever age; try for the biggest goals we can set our sights on. These are only limited by our imagination. Failure is only in not starting.

There are no boundaries to what we can try to achieve. As you can see from my attempts throughout life, not everything is going to be a success, but it's sure fun giving it all a go. And any failures to finish don't define us, but help to make us stronger for the next attempt at the same or different goals and, as such, are not failures, just steps towards who we want to be.

I was reading the other day about a young American woman who has attempted to run a hundred-mile race through mountainous country four times and has failed at each one. In her second attempt, she got as far as eighty miles before she was pulled from the course with severe dehydration. I don't know anything about that lady but I can't see her efforts as failures; rather, I see brave attempts to do something she had dreamed about achieving for years. For that, I truly admire her and would argue with anyone that she did not fail or come anywhere near failing. Even just trying is winning.

Sometimes, my training runs are cut short because, on that particular day, I am lacking something: sometimes it's motivation, other times the weather stops me or I sense that an injury may be coming along. Perhaps I have time restraints because of community commitments. But they are runs and they are achieving something, even if it is simply knowing myself a little better.

In getting to know myself better in recent years, after all my trials and tribulations, I have had to accept that a fair chunk of ultra marathon races are beyond my capabilities. It has been a difficult situation to look at eye to eye but, in reality, I have had no choice.

For instance, many events cross high mountain ranges in Nepal or wild parts of America that sound absolutely amazing and really strike a chord within me. Clearly, these would be wonderful places to run but they are now beyond even my wildest dreams.

I was most disappointed to miss out on the 1984 Six Foot Track Race. This was the inaugural version of that ultra trail race through the Blue Mountains west of Sydney. The original organisers were great people I had met at several marathons. They had been expounding on the beauty of the course, which was to finish at the renowned Jenolan Caves deep in the mountains.

I was fully trained for the run and even got as far as the overnight motel, near the starting point at the Explorers' Tree in Blackheath. An early bedtime was to set me up for a feel-good kind of day, but when I woke in the middle of the night with a raging sore throat and throbbing head, I realised that it would take all my effort to just climb out of bed. There was no way that I would be able to run five kilometres, let alone more than sixty. 'Oh, well,' I thought, 'I can always run it next year.'

Somehow, it sadly never fitted in with my schedule over the next few years and, by the time I was ready and desperate to run it, the race directors (ironically the Sydney Striders with whom I had run so many years ago) had introduced strict cut-off times that I was now too slow to make. Ah well, another one bites the dust.

The most wonderful event I could ever imagine running is the Badwater 135. This amazing one-hundred-and-thirty-five-mile (two-hundred-and-fifteen-kilometre) race takes place in Death Valley, California, (the lowest spot in the USA) and is run at the hottest time of the year (it can get up to fifty-five degrees) when the soles of shoes melt on the tarmac and runners constantly need to be sprayed with cold water or even put into ice baths. Yet the applications to enter far exceed the number of places available. The cost of race entry, including the requirement that you have two support vehicles and a substantial crew, is exorbitant. But some runners have completed it on ten separate occasions.

So what is the reason for such intense interest in this cruel event? People want to test themselves and their limits, but this race goes beyond that I think. Death Valley is extraordinary and the conditions so extreme that it has been called the hardest race on earth – and that will always attract the extreme athletes. The event just blows my mind. I just love watching one of the many videos about the race (*Racing On the Sun* is my favourite), and will always be disappointed that I wasn't anywhere near good enough, or wealthy enough, to get a guernsey into Badwater.

Some years ago, I had the opportunity to run some of the Badwater course when we were driving through Death Valley and, boy, was it brutally tough. The utterly dry air made me feel as if I wasn't sweating, although it was nearly fifty degrees Celsius and, after an hour or so, the water in my bottle was far too warm to drink. I was desperate to get back to the motel where we were staying in Stovepipe Wells. My lungs were burning and it felt almost impossible to draw breath. My legs were desperate for oxygen that my lungs weren't delivering. I shuffled along like an old desperado searching for gold in the dusty sand blown over the road by the hot, dry wind.

About three kilometres from the motel, a car pulled up and a man jumped out and told me he was making a video about California for a German TV show. He wanted to take some footage of me running across the desert. All I can say is that he must have been desperately short of material. I said OK, but secretly I was quite worried about staying out there any longer. I managed to keep going as he thrust a movie camera out of his car window, driving alongside me. The heat was making me giddy, I was weaving around on the road a little and all I wanted was a cold shower and an air conditioner. But looking back on that Death Valley experience, it was all the richer for such a silly episode.

As time flies past and I realistically face up to the body limitations that I now have, I am thinking of doing more and more self-organised runs where I can shuffle along a pre-planned route in my own time, stopping wherever I find a suitable spot. Apart from being able to do things at my own pace, I will have the added pleasure of spending time planning new routes.

Of course, I ran/walked the Great Southern Rail Trail with friends, but I have also had in mind for a while now running solo around Port Phillip Bay in Melbourne. The plan is to carry a minimal backpack, buy food along the way and stop at motels or pubs where I can. I have been studying the map for ages and think I can do the circuit in four easy days, but if it takes five that's no problem, just another fun day out there. Mind you, I haven't broached that particular outing with my wife yet, but I'll be sure to stress what a good opportunity it will be for me to see some of our widespread family.

But, of course, sharing an adventure with others is even better. One of the attractions is that you can talk about running – runs you have done in the past, as well as future goals – without boring your fellow travellers. You know what it's like when non-running friends or acquaintances ask you what you're up to. When you start to describe your last fifty-miler or twenty-four-hour race, a glazed look comes into their eyes and you know it's time to change the subject.

Consequently, it has worked out that I have two sets of friends, one in the ordinary part of my life and the other on 'the dark side' – runners who care about what I am doing and I in their achievements and ambitions. I am not an especially great fan of social media but I have found that staying in touch with running friends and groups on Facebook allows each of us to support the efforts and successes others are accomplishing. This community connection will always remain important to me.

When I think about sharing, I am certainly looking forward to having running adventures with my son Steve, who has already completed several marathons and is just starting to discover trail running. In a way, I sense that he has a bit of his father's obsessiveness in him. He is constantly checking out running events that he would like to enter. I often get text messages highlighting upcoming races he is thinking about. Father and son adventures sound very appealing.

In his book *What I Talk About When I Talk About Running*, Haruki Murakami wrote, 'The honour of physical decline is waiting (for each of us), and you have to get used to that reality.' We do need to feel comfortable in our ageing skin, but it would be a great pity if we did not at least try to resist the downward spiral of ageing. We should make the most we can of each and every day.

Dylan Thomas wrote darkly about the end of our lives in probably his most famous poem.

> Do not go gentle into that good night.
> Old age should burn and rave at close of day;
> Rage, rage against the dying of the light.

I love Thomas's poems and this one in particular has, since I was a young man, come to me when I have thought about getting older. It served to remind me that life is for living and his somewhat loud yelp of rage wouldn't let me forget it. Especially now, it is an important poem to keep reading. So, please, rage, rage against the dying of the light every day.

In spite of everything, I certainly won't rest on my laurels, but will, forever more, be setting myself tough goals. At the same time, I know I have to accept that there may be limits – only I fight hard against them being imposed upon me by external factors. So I keep on swimming against the current and will continue to submit entry forms to races/adventures that appeal to me but scare me at the same time.

It is so easy to choose not to do anything outside of your comfort zone, but deciding to do so will empower you tremendously and change your life dramatically forever. The important thing is getting out and doing something physical rather than being a mere spectator. And, equally important, we need to be absorbed by what we choose to do. In doing so, we find a kind of freedom – freedom from the mundane and ugly side of life that we encounter now and then.

As human beings, we can change the way we live during our short time here on Earth. As a younger man, I was very fortunate to realise that my dissolute life was causing the wheels to fall off and I was heading for disaster. While it wasn't easy, I was able to claw my way slowly back on track through hard work and self-discipline. The easy, quick fix solution doesn't exist, even though that's what we'd all like. It took me quite a while and strong determination to get as fit and healthy as I could be.

Writing this book has certainly helped me to see myself more clearly. It has also helped me to be proud of my achievements, but to recognise how little they mean in the overall scheme of things. I have only to see what others have done to overcome horrible setbacks that life has thrown at them to make me realise how minor mine have been.

So I really hope that all OFRs and, indeed, budding OFRs, will look up at the stars and reach out to them. We can run our hearts out or just lie in bed and rot.

I hope that I see you out there on the trails with a smile on your face.

23

Mirror, Mirror, on the Wall

'I'll be happy if running and I can grow old together.' – Haruki Murakami

I strive to be many things. The perfect person operating out of an ageing body. Naturally, I have failed big time; fallen below the standards that I have aspired to. It's a bit like running, I guess. I set my goals as high as I can, try to get there but have to accept the reality of what I achieve. No matter what, I believe that we need a distinct purpose if we want to live a full life.

Sometimes, it seems that I have spread myself too thinly across a multitude of areas, rather than trying to achieve more in fewer disciplines. But that's me. I can't change my basic characteristics, so I will just keep on running up that hill, sometimes pushing a rather large boulder.

On the brighter side, however, because I am a runner,
I get to see my friends without their clothes on.
I have the pleasure of mixing travel with running. Or is it vice versa?
I have met so many people who have had a positive influence on my life.
I get to explore the local bush tracks with my dog Suzie.
I have a passion in life that I can focus on when I need to.
I have more positive energy for other aspects of life.
I get to spend money on some pretty funky running gear.
I know how to get lost on the trails at night.
I get to see amazing wilderness regions in various parts of the world.
I am content with my own company for long periods.

I use my obsession to raise money for worthwhile charities.

I know that I'm not going to get any faster but I just love doing it.

I get more value for money in races, being slow.

I love seeing our children and grandchildren get into running.

I get pleasure from motivating others. If I can do it, so can they.

Of course, throughout our lives we are constantly striving for acceptance, approval, love, wealth and the ever-illusive 'happiness'. Now, at seventy-four years old, I can be extremely happy with the fact that from now on running is purely the pleasure of being out on the trails. But, while I am grateful that I have love in my life, I don't know about the approval or wealth bits. Overall, though, things have worked out better than I could have hoped.

I might still be a little too ambitious in my running expectations but why not? Reality keeps me in check by reminding me that, although I will never totally accept a smaller slice of the adventure pie, I now have only a modest sized plate to eat from.

Oh yes – how fortunate I have been to find running.

Appendix

My favourite running books

The Complete Book of Running – James F. Fixx (Random House, 1977)
Running and Being – George Sheehan (Simon & Schuster, 1978)
Born To Run – Christopher McDougall (Alfred A. Knopf, 2009)
Ultra Marathon Man – Dean Karnazes (Penguin Grooup, 2005)
Duel in the Sun – John Brant (Rodale Inc., 2006)
To the Edge – Kirk Johnson (Warner Books, 2001)

My favourite podcasts

Find Your Feet
Running In the Centre of the Universe
Ginger Runner Live
Casefile True Crime
Books & Authors
Sam Gash

My favourite motivational speakers

Hanny Allston
Pat Farmer
Steve Moneghetti
Sam Gash

My favourite running gear shops (in Tasmania)

Find Your Feet (Hobart and Launceston) – www.findyourfeet.com
The Running Company, Launceston

My favourite race websites

www.rapidascent.com.au (Larapinta multi-day race)
www.global events.com (Cambodia, Bhutan and Albania multi-day races)
www.taraweraultra.com.nz
www.flindersislandrunningfestival.com.au (famous Pub2Pub)

My favourite post-race beers

Big Red Run – Iron Jack
Cambodia – Angkor
Flinders Island Running Festival – Boag's Draught
Larapinta – anything from Alice Springs Brewing Co.
Launceston Marathon – Morrison's Pale Ale
Tarawera – Enduro Pale Ale

Acknowledgements

Firstly, many thanks to all those who so generously sponsored my charity fund raising runs over the years, including
The wonderful Flinders Island community
Bendigo & Rural Bank
CBM Sustainability
Flinders Council
Flinders Island Sports & RSL Club
Godfrey Pembroke (Launceston)
Launceston Kitchen Centre
Nichols Poultry
Sharp Airlines
Specsavers
Tasports
Vos Construction.

Without your amazing support, the runs wouldn't have happened and the charities that benefited would have been worse off.

Obviously, without the assistance, great ideas and loving spirit of my wife Dale I would have struggled to get this book completed. So thank you, darling. I love you very much.

Special thanks go to son Steve Williams for sharing some of my adventures. There's many more to come, young fella. And also to daughter Vicki for her continual enthusiastic support.

To my brother Geoff – thanks for your constant encouragement.

Thanks also go to our island physiotherapist, David Heap, for keeping my oldish body from falling apart and enabling me to complete so many races.

I really appreciate the great photos that Sammi Goldthorpe and Angela Smith allowed me to use.

Many thanks to great friends Kim and Spud Murphy who, among other support, looked after our dog Suzie when I was out running off the island.

I have received great advice and editorial services from Anthony Reeder for which I am indebted.

And, finally, to all the friends that I have shared the roads and trails with – thank you so much for all you have given me.

About the Author

Apart from running as often and as far as possible, David has lived with his wife Dale on remote Flinders Island in the wild Bass Strait for the past twenty years. In his spare time, David is deputy mayor of the local council and has served on council for over fifteen years. He also does voluntary work at the golf club and in the fire brigade.

Before going to Flinders Island, his career was in the financial industry, working at a desk in Sydney. When their five children had left home, it was time for Dale and David to find new adventures in life. The first thing David did was to start an antiquarian bookshop in Sydney. Books have been a lifelong passion. After a few years, the attraction of a more remote life took hold when he and his wife discovered Flinders Island.

Over his forty years of running, David has completed well over a hundred marathons, including more than twenty ultra marathons (42.2+ kilometres) as well as a myriad of smaller races, plus yearly efforts in the Mothers' Day Classic with several of the nine grandkids who keep him out of mischief.

The ultra marathons include a couple of twenty-four-hour races round a track as well as some multi-day events in wild, wild places such as the Simpson Desert, the McDonnell Ranges and Cambodia.

Over the years, David has raised in excess of $30,000 for cancer research by running from one end of Flinders Island to the other (seventy-six kilometres) twice, and from Launceston to Hobart.

David enjoys growing most of his own vegetables and takes the opportunity whenever he can to catch fish for dinner. He thrives on the lifestyle that living on Flinders Island brings.

www.ingramcontent.com/pod-product-compliance
Lightning Source LLC
Chambersburg PA
CBHW070901080526
44589CB00013B/1157